COLLINS GEM

WHISKY

THIRD EDITION

Carol P. Shaw

HarperCollins*Publishers*

HarperCollins Publishers
PO Box, Glasgow G4 0NB

First published 1993
Second Edition 1995
Third Edition 1997

Reprint 9 8 7 6 5 4 3 2 1 0

ISBN 0 00 472120 9

The Author and Publishers would like to thank all the
distillers, independent bottlers and trade associations
who kindly assisted in the preparation of information
and material for this book.

Printed in Italy by Amadeus S.p.A.

CONTENTS

The Whiskies of Scotland

Taste Rating 64

INTRODUCTION

These are by no means easy times for the whisky industry. Faced with the threat of the abolition of the lucrative duty-free scheme in 1999, and a competition in the drinks industry which is continually re-inventing both itself and new brands, Scotch whisky has a hard fight on its hands to maintain its market share.

Yet there are reasons for optimism: the long-established trend of distillery closures has recently shown signs of reversal, with the re-opening of mothballed distilleries – Glengarioch and Ardbeg being a case in point – and even the setting up of new ventures, as at Lochranza on Arran.

The fact that this is the third edition of Collins *Gem Whisky* is also proof that whisky continues to attract many and interested followers, from those with experienced palates, who have very definite ideas on what they like and often are prepared to pay plenty to get it, to beginners, who possibly feel intimidated by the range and breadth of choice available and are unsure of where to start. For this latter group, I offer a word of advice: don't be afraid to experiment. Whisky-drinking is not the sole preserve of the stuffy or of middle-aged males, and neither is it strung up by snobbish attitudes. There is no single way it has to be served, and no esoteric knowledge is needed to enjoy it. Mix it with anything you like – it is an acquired taste – but get to know it on your own terms. Too many women and young people seem to miss out on what can be a sublime experience and a life-long pleasure because whisky is felt to have an off-putting mystique. Hopefully, this book will continue to make its pleasures more accessible to all enthusiasts across the whole range of experience.

Slàinte mhath!

THE HISTORY OF SCOTCH WHISKY-MAKING

It is widely accepted that whisky has been distilled in Scotland for hundreds of years, and different hypotheses as to its origins have been suggested. Some state that it was brought into the country by missionary monks from Ireland; others point out that, as the Arabs were among the first to learn distillation techniques, knights and men returning from the Crusades could have brought the knowledge back with them. It may well be, however, that it evolved simply as a means of using up barley which would otherwise have been ruined after a wet harvest.

A good supply of water is a prerequisite for distilling (Glenmorangie)

The name itself is derived from the Gaelic, *uisge beatha*, meaning 'water of life'. The Latin equivalent, *aqua vitae*, was a term which was commonly used throughout Europe to describe the local spirit. *Aqua vitae* made its first appearance in official Scottish records in 1494, with the record of malt being sold to one Friar John Cor with which to make the spirit, but *uisge* seems to have first been mentioned in the account of the funeral and wake

of a Highland chieftain around 1618. The amount of whisky making throughout Scotland increased greatly during the seventeenth century, and nowhere more so than in the Highlands. In fact, so enthusiastic was the growth in distillation that before the end of the six-teenth century there had already been complaints in Parliament that so much barley was being used in whisky production that it was in short supply as a foodstuff! These distillers' method was basic and simple: a sack of barley might be soaked in water – for example, in a burn

– for a day or two, then the barley would be spread out in a dry place, allowing it to sprout, for around 10 days. The sprouting would be halted by drying the barley over a peat fire (peat being used as the main source of fuel in the Highlands). It was then put in a container with boiling water and yeast, to ferment. This mix would be passed twice through a pot still, emerging as whisky at the other end. These distillers had to be fairly skilled at their job, to possess the judgement to know when to take off the middle cut of the spirit (the drinkable part), avoiding the poisonous foreshots, at the start of the distillation, and the lower-quality feints, or aftershots, at the end. Although they had no instruments, methods did evolve of testing the whisky's strength, including setting fire to the spirit to measure the amount of liquid left behind, and mixing it with gunpowder to see how it reacted when ignited – if the gunpowder-and-whisky cocktail exploded, it was known that the whisky was too strong!

It was during the seventeenth century, too, that the first tax on whisky was introduced by Parliament, because of the pressing need to raise revenue to finance the army fighting in the English Civil War in 1644. Although it was reduced under the Commonwealth, this episode effectively marked the beginning of the principle of the taxation of whisky.

The union of Scotland and England in 1707, however, heralded some changes for the whisky industry, and few of them were constructive. A malt tax was introduced in 1725 which adversely affected the quality of beer – until then the most popular drink – and of whiskies produced by the professional

Sir Edward Landseer's somewhat romanticised view of an illicit still in the Highlands (United Distillers)

commercial distillers in the more populous Lowlands, who were obliged to produce whiskies of poorer quality, with less malted barley content. These taxes also applied to Highland malt whisky, but in that still-inaccessible region it was much easier to ignore, and illicit distillation continued to flourish. This attempt at revenue raising, affecting the Lowland distillers but ignored in the Highlands, set a pattern for the rest of the century.

The large distillers in the Lowlands continued successfully to produce rough grain whisky whose quantity was more important than its quality, for consumption locally and in England, where it was often used as a basis for cheap gin. However, pressure from the English distillers, who were being undercut by Scottish imports flooding the market, encouraged Parliament to introduce a series of increasingly draconian taxes against the Scots whisky. The small distillers in the Highlands – most of whom were probably farmers and crofters, pursuing a lucrative sideline – continued to make superior quality whisky without paying tax. Much of this whisky was brought to the Lowlands for sale, where it was more popular with those who could afford it than the rougher spirit produced by the Lowland distillers. The government in London had no answer to the problems they had helped create in the whisky industry, other than to raise taxes still further, making the law seem more and more ineffectual.

Finally, however, pressure on the government brought an abandonment of its futile attempts at taxation and regulation. A Royal Commission was set up to investigate the industry, the Excise service in the Highlands was strengthened, and in 1822 an act was passed which brought harsher penalties for those found to be operating unlicensed stills. The following year the Excise Act made an attempt to encourage licensed distilling, cutting both duty and restrictions on exports to England. Now, an annual licence of £10 was introduced on stills over forty gallons (smaller stills were not allowed), and a more modest duty of 2/3d per gallon of whisky brought in. The Duke of Gordon, whose estates included the Glenlivet area, was a prime mover in the reforms, and he encouraged his tenants, including George Smith, producer of the whisky which came to be known as The Glenlivet, to take out licences. The new act was effective and successful, and the amount of legally distilled whisky consumed had risen threefold by 1827.

Freed from its legislative shackles, the whisky industry was able to concentrate on the development of its product and markets. The product itself was given an impetus by the invention by Aeneas Coffey, an Irish former exciseman, of a new still which he patented in 1832; this allowed the distillation of grain whisky to take place in a continuous process in one still. The new process cut back on costs, allowing the Lowland grain distillers to use even less malted barley than before, and to produce on an even bigger scale. Ironically, however, the success of the Excise Act and the new patent still brought trouble for the industry during the mid nineteenth century, because of overproduction and despite the exploiting of new export markets in the Empire and overseas. This development saw the foreshadowing of the emergence of the Distillers Company, with the combining in a price-fixing cartel of the six biggest Lowland grain whisky producers; they were not to join together officially, however, until 1877, by which time the face of the industry had changed dramatically.

This change was brought about by the development of techniques of blending malt and grain whiskies to produce a lighter spirit than the traditional single malt, and a more flavoursome one than grain whisky. In the 1850s Andrew Usher, the Edinburgh whisky merchant who was agent for the Glenlivet whiskies, had vatted together several casks of Glenlivet from his stocks, producing in the process a more consistent product. The practice was soon extended to the blending of malt and grain.

One of Andrew Usher's blends

This was held to produce a lighter spirit which English drinkers, unused to the much stronger malt product of the pot still, found much more palatable. It also introduced an element of consistency to the product. Coincidentally, this development came when reserves of brandy, the first-choice spirit in England, were threatened as a result of the Phylloxera blight in the French vineyards in the 1860s. Timely exploitation of the market in England by the grain producers and blenders meant that, as stocks of brandy declined in the 1870s and '80s, the new blended whiskies came to take their place as the quality spirit, and the 1890s was a period of unprecedented growth for the Scottish whisky industry. New malt distilleries were opened and groups like Distillers and the North British Distillery Company, serving the interests of the grain distillers and the blenders respectively, became phenomenally successful. The whisky industry was developing to become recognizable as the industry it is today.

The boom period was followed, typically, by a slump, and difficult times for the industry at the beginning of this century were compounded by the First World War and the introduction of Prohibition in the USA in 1920. The years from then to the Second World War saw a drop in output of almost 50%, and an almost complete halt being brought to the production of malt whisky. This situation continued after the war when, naturally, what grain was available had to be diverted to feed the people rather than make whisky. As prosperity returned in the 1950s, whisky output increased and exports rose. New distilleries were built in the 1960s, old ones reopened, and the production of malt whisky quadrupled in a decade. Take-over and consolidation were the keynotes of the industry in the 1970s, with English brewers moving into the whisky market on a large scale. This trend culminated in the messy take-over of the Distillers Company (now United Distillers) by Guinness, a transaction which resulted in the chairman of the brewing giant and several of his advisers ending up in court. Ironically, however, the adage of there being no bad publicity seems to be borne out by the Distillers take-over: an episode which apparently brought the industry into disrepute, came at a time when the market was picking up again after the slump lasting from the mid '70s to the mid '80s, and served to give whisky a timely publicity boost.

This upturn in the drink's fortunes continued into the 1990s, with the emphasis in marketing being placed on quality rather than quantity: cheaper blends have tended to disappear, single malts are taking an increasing share of the market, and price rises are being met by consumers, who seem to prefer the new expensive-and-exclusive image of the drink. Increasing importance was placed on packaging and advertising, and with the marketing of new visitor centres in the distilleries themselves as tourist attractions in their own right. By 1995, however, growth in the Scotch market as a whole had slowed once again and the industry was having to work hard to maintain its position. The premium end of the industry continued to be healthy (helped no doubt by the first reduction in excise duty for a hundred years) although the mass-market sector faced increasing competition, particularly from vodka producers. It responded by the creation of whisky-based drinks designed to appeal to a younger, less traditional customer base – whiskies spiked with red chilli peppers, for example – but the long-term success of these remains to be seen. Perhaps the biggest challenge facing the drinks industry as it moves towards the new millennium is the abandonment of duty-free facilities within the European Union in 1999; this will be a particularly harsh blow to the Scotch producers to whom the duty-free market is worth some £80 million. The industry has faced other crises before and it will undoubtedly survive this one and flourish once more – something which can only be good for all those who appreciate and love good whisky.

Lochranze Distillery on the Iselof Arran. Opened in 1995, it is one of Scotland's newest distilleries (Isle of Arran Distillery Ltd)

HOW SCOTCH WHISKY IS MADE

Two different processes are used for the distillation of Scotch malt and grain whiskies.

MALT WHISKY

In malt whisky distillation, there are several basic steps to the process: malting, mashing, fermentation, distillation and maturation, although the minor elements may vary from one distillery to another. Barley may be bought in pre-malted, but if it is not, it is first filtered to remove any foreign matter.

Barley (Glenmorangie plc)

Malting

The process begins when the barley is transferred to soak in tanks of water which go by the self-explanatory name of barley steeps; this process takes two to four days. In the traditional process, the barley is then spread on a malting floor, to be turned by hand daily for the next twelve days or so, allowing it to sprout; now, however, most distilleries use mechanical devices for turning the sprouting barley. As the seeds germinate, the starch in the barley releases some of its sugars. At the appropriate moment, germination is stopped by drying the cereal in a malt kiln over a peat furnace or fire. The peat smoke which flavours the drying barley at this stage

Turning the barley by hand on a traditional malting floor (Scotch Whisky Association)

Adding peat to the kiln (Glenmorangie plc)

A traditional pagoda-topped malting kiln (Scotch Whisky Association)

can, depending on its intensity, be tasted in the final whisky itself. The malt kilns traditionally had the pagoda-style roofs which were such an instantly recognizable characteristic of the malt distilleries; these can still be seen on older distilleries.

Mashing

The next stage for the malted barley is passage through a mill, from which it emerges roughly ground as grist. From here it is moved to a mash tun, a large vat where it is mixed with hot water and agitated, so that its sugars dissolve to produce wort, a sweet, non-alcoholic liquid. This process is repeated to ensure that all the sugars have been collected. The solid remains of the barley are removed at this point for conversion to cattle food.

Producing the wort in the mash tun (Glenmorangie plc)

Washbacks where the wort is fermented to produce the wash (Scotch Whisky Association)

Fermentation

The wort is cooled and transferred to washbacks, large vats where yeast is added and the process of fermentation begins. The chemical reaction which takes place with the addition of the yeast converts the sugars in the wort to alcohol, a process which takes around two days and results in a low-strength alcoholic liquid now called wash.

Distillation

The wash is then ready for the stills. The shape of the still is one of the most important factors in the whisky-making

HOW SCOTCH WHISKY IS MADE

process, as it can have a decisive influence on the final character of the malt whisky: for instance, a still with a short neck will produce a whisky with heavier oils and a more intense flavour, whereas lighter-flavoured whiskies with less heavy oils will emerge from a still with a long or high neck. The first still which the wash passes through is known, appropriately, as the wash still, and here it is heated. As the alcohol has a lower boiling point than water, the alcoholic steam rises up

Copper wash stills (Scotch Whisky Association)

the still through its long spout to the worm, a condensing coil. The distillate, now called low wines, is passed into the second still, the spirit still, where the process is repeated, with the liquid running off into the glass-fronted spirit safe.

It is at this point that the skill of the distiller is crucial: unable to smell or taste the liquid to judge it, he must know when to separate the middle cut, or main run of the spirit, which contains the best-quality alcohol needed for malt

How malt whisky is made

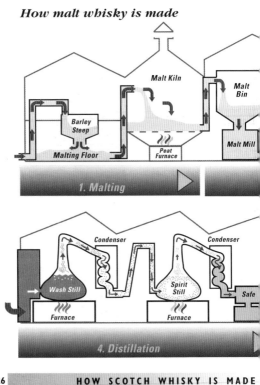

Malt Kiln

Malt Bin

Barley Steep

Malting Floor

Peat Furnace

Malt Mill

1. Malting

Condenser

Condenser

Wash Still

Spirit Still

Furnace

Furnace

Safe

4. Distillation

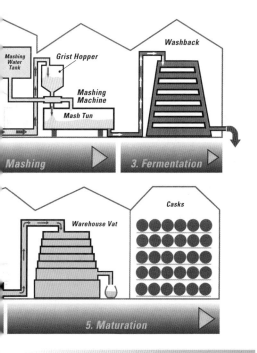

Mashing Water Tank

Grist Hopper

Washback

Mashing Machine

Mash Tun

Mashing

3. Fermentation

Warehouse Vat

Casks

5. Maturation

whisky, from the foreshots (the raw, poisonous first distillate) and the feints, or aftershots, which contain a lower grade of alcohol. Once separated, foreshots and feints are fed back into the wash for redistillation.

Drawing off a sample of the new whisky from the spirit sample safe (Glenturret Distillery Ltd)

Maturation

The main run of the alcohol is now transferred for storage to a vat and is mixed with water to bring it down in strength. It is then transferred into casks for maturing. The whole process of distillation can theoretically be completed inside a week, but the whisky must now mature for at least three years before it can be sold; during this time, a small percentage of the whisky, known as the 'angels' share', will evaporate. In practice, malt whiskies are left to mature for an average of eight to fifteen years.

GRAIN WHISKY

With the exception of the Invergordon Distillery, all grain distilleries are located in the Lowlands. Grain distilleries use patent (or Coffey) stills, which can operate continuously. The basic process used is similar to that for malt, up to the point of distillation, although everything takes place on a much larger scale, and with much less malted barley: maize, unmalted barley or other cereals are generally used.

Maturing casks (Glenturret Distillery Ltd)

Distillation is carried out in two large cylindrical columns which are linked by pipes. The wash passes into the first column, the rectifier, in a coiled pipe running through its length. Jets of steam are forced up into the column, through a series of perforated plates between which the coiled pipe passes, heating the wash inside before it passes out and into the analyser. In the analyser the wash is no longer in the coiled pipe, and it is now met by another jet of steam passing through more perforated plates. The steam and evaporated alcohol rise and are passed back into the rectifier, with the alcohol cooling as it moves up, encountering fresh, cold wash in the coiled pipe on its way down, until it reaches a cold water coil where it condenses before passing out of the still. The impure alcohols in the first and last part of the distillate can be redistilled, while the alcohol which reaches the spirit safe and receiver is very pure. The whisky will mature faster than malt, and is less subject to variable factors. The vast majority of the produce will go for blending not long after its three-year maturation period has passed.

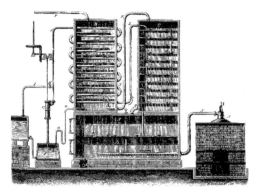

A detail from an 1870 illustration showing the internal workings of the Coffey Still

BLENDING

Blending is a slightly separate part of the whisky-making process, with a third product being made from malt and grain whiskies. It both guarantees consistency of the brand and aims to create a new whisky of character in its own right. It is a process which absorbs the greater part of the distilleries' production, and is the mainstay of the industry.

The process was developed on a commercial footing in the second half of the nineteenth century. Although it may initially have been used as a way of stretching further supplies of the more expensive malt whisky, it was the means by which whisky was popularized first in the English market, then overseas.

The blender at work (Scotch Whisky Association)

Blending is an olfactory craft, with blenders nosing rather than tasting whiskies. It is a highly skilled profession, with anything from 20 to 50 different whiskies being mixed in any one brand, including varieties of type, region, distillery and age. The new whisky's character is dependent on how well

BLENDING

these different component whiskies complement and contrast with one another to bring out their various flavours. The high number of component whiskies is the blender's guarantee of consistency: if one contributing distillery goes out of production, the consistency of the blend can be maintained

The ultimate blend: J&B Ultima combines 116 malt and 12 grain whiskies.

more easily than if there were a lesser number of whiskies, each with a stronger presence, as ingredients.

The ingredients and their proportions are closely guarded secrets, although it is generally assumed that where a blender owns a distillery, the distillery's produce will be represented to some degree in the blend: so, for example, the produce of Laphroaig Distillery, which is owned by Allied Distillers, is present in their Long John, Ballantine's and Teacher's blends. The produce of some distilleries is never bottled as a single malt, and goes entirely for blending.

After the whiskies are matured, they are mixed together in their correct proportions in a vat, then 'married' in oak casks for at least a year to allow intermingling and further maturation to take place. As with most malts, the blend is reduced to the correct strength by the addition of water. Burnt-sugar caramel may be added to bring a blend up to its desired colour before the whisky is filtered, bottled and labelled.

DIFFERENT TYPES OF SCOTCH WHISKY

There are particular legal constraints on what can be termed Scotch whisky, the most basic of which dictate the components of the whisky (cereals, malt and yeast), the maximum alcoholic strength at distillation (94.8% alcohol by volume), and the minimum length of maturation (at least three years). Finally, the whisky itself must have been distilled and matured in Scotland.

Scotland produces two main types of whisky, and all the available varieties of the spirit are variations on these themes. The first is malt whisky, made from malted barley, using a pot still; and the second is grain whisky, made from other cereals – maize or unmalted barley, together with a little malted barley – in a patent still. The two types' distillation processes are explained on pp. 20–30; what follows here is an explanation of the varieties in which they are available.

SINGLE MALT WHISKIES

Single malt whisky is the product of one distillery. Legally, it can be sold after only three years' maturation, but in practice it is generally left to mature from between eight to fifteen years, by which time its character and flavour has become more pronounced and rounded. Generally, whiskies of varying proof strengths and ages from different casks are mixed together,

The Macallan and Glenfiddich: two of the most popular single malts

ensuring a consistent distillery product (as the product of any one distillation will inevitably not be identical to any other), although the age which appears on the label is always the age of the youngest distillation in the bottle. Malts are diluted from their cask strength (up to mid 60s percentage alcohol by volume) to 40% or 43% for commercial marketing. Single malts comprise a relatively small, although increasing, proportion of the total whisky market.

Single cask whiskies

A sub-group of single malt whisky is the single-cask malt. Generally available commercially only through specialist shops and independent merchants (see pp. 53–55), these are whiskies

DIFFERENT TYPES

which, as the name suggests, are the produce of one distillation, bottled straight from the cask and not vatted with any other produce from the distillery. This process, together with the absence of chill filtration before the whiskies are bottled, ensures that the particular character of a distillery's whisky – and, indeed, of a specific distillation – is unmasked, and greatly emphasized. Supplies of a particular

A typical Cadenhead's single cask bottling of a single malt

variety or distillation are, by nature, finite. This is the most expensive type of whisky, often costing at least double the price of a normal, distillery-bottled single malt, but felt by many whisky drinkers to be well worth the expense.

Vatted malt whiskies

A vatted malt is the final of the malt whisky sub-groups. This type of whisky has a long pedigree, having formed the basis of the first blended whisky in the mid nineteenth century. Vatted malts are normally produced by blenders and big companies who have a variety of malt distilleries from which to take their product. It could be regarded as a half-way house between a blend and a single malt, although the flavours in some vatted malts can be just as well developed as those in a single. Single malts of different distilleries and different ages are mixed together, the age (if any) on the label being that of the youngest whisky in the mixture. The words 'vatted malt' normally do not appear on a label; instead, the absence of the word 'single' before 'malt', together with an absence of a distillery name, is generally an indicator of a vatted malt.

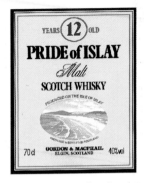

A vatted malt prroduced by independent bottlers, Gordon & MacPhail

Grain whiskies

Grain whisky has been mentioned briefly above, and in proportion to the quantities in which it is produced, very little is bottled in its own right. Instead, its main function is as a component part of a blend.

The Invergordon, one of the few grain whiskies generally available

DIFFERENT TYPES

Blended whiskies

Blended whiskies are a mixture of malt and grain, not necessarily in any fixed proportions but rather in a recipe which will achieve the blender's desired balance in terms of character, cost and quality. Blends were the means in the nineteenth century by which hitherto too-strongly flavoured malt whiskies were mellowed for the palate in markets outside Scotland – firstly for England, then for export markets. The desired aim of a blender is not to dilute or diminish the flavours of the various component whiskies, but rather to choose ones which are both compatible

Two of the most famous –and popular – blends throughout the world

and complementary, resulting in the creation of a new whisky of distinctive character. In this way, consistency of the product can also be assured. Blended whiskies, of which there are over a thousand, comprise the greater part of the whisky market. The major blenders generally own both malt and grain distilleries, so it is safe to assume that the product of a particular malt distillery will be represented to some degree in its owner's blends.

De luxe whiskies

A de luxe whisky is a particular type of blend, recognized to be of superior quality to a standard blend. De luxe whiskies generally contain a higher proportion of malt which is older, more mature and consequently more expensive. Some de luxes carry an age statement on their label; as with other whiskies, this is the age of the youngest component in the bottle.

Blends, but of a quite different type, is a name which can be given

The very distinctive de luxe, Dimple

to the growing market for whisky liqueurs. Some of these contain whisky flavoured with honey, fruits, herbs and spices, while the cream liqueurs also contain whisky, but are more inclined towards cream, coffee and chocolate in their flavours.

REGIONAL CHARACTERISTICS OF SCOTCH MALT WHISKY

The qualities and characteristics associated with particular producing regions are not a result of current tastes and fashions, but rather a legacy of the past. In times when roads were often poor or, at some times of the year, non-existent, when communications were often difficult, sometimes dangerous and always time-consuming, and trade between different parts of the country was expensive, it was obvious that a distillery would use the raw materials and ingredients which were to hand in a particular locality rather than go to the trouble of importing produce from other areas. These factors, combined with local climate and geology, helped produce whiskies which varied in character from oné part of the country to another.

The current chief distinction, between Highland and Lowland whiskies, is also a legacy of a past legal and fiscal policy. As a means of controlling the trade and movement of whisky from the Highlands to the Lowlands (whose cheaper, coarser grain spirit was then successfully being exported into England), the Highland dividing line was established, following roughly the Highland Boundary Fault Line, which runs from the Firth of Clyde to the Firth of Tay. The distinction remained, even with the equalizing of quality between malts from north and south of the line, and is still recognized today. The maps on pp. 42–43 and 48–49 show all existing distilleries within the broad categorizations that follow.

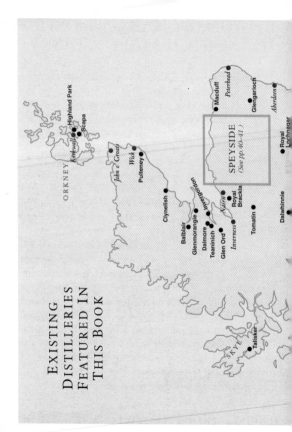

EXISTING
DISTILLERIES
FEATURED IN
THIS BOOK

ORKNEY

Kirkwall Highland Park
Scapa

Wick
John o' Groats Pulteney

Clynelish

Balblair
Glenmorangie Invergordon
Dalmore
Teaninich Nairn Macduff Peterhead
Glen Ord Royal Glengarioch
Inverness Brackla Aberdeen
Tomatin

SPEYSIDE
(See pp. 40-41)

Royal
Lochnagar
Dalwhinnie

SKYE

Talisker

LOWLAND

Lowland malts are defined as those coming from the southern half of Scotland – that is, from south of the Highland line. In terms of their taste, the Lowland malts are perhaps a good first stepping stone into the wider world of malt whiskies for the drinker who wants to graduate from blends: relatively unassertive in character, they are generally soft and light, with a gentle sweetness which ensures them many fans among more experienced palates. Much of the produce of the Lowland malt distilleries is used in blends.

CAMPBELTOWN

As a once-popular music-hall ditty more colourfully suggested, Campbeltown was a major centre of whisky production. Over twenty distilleries operated there in the later nineteenth century, encouraged by the abundance of local supplies of peat, barley from the Mull of Kintyre, and a nearby source of cheap coal. However, over-production, too-wide variations in quality and the exhaustion of the local coal seam contributed to the decline of the local industry, to the point where only two distilleries now remain. With the shift in emphasis from sea-borne to road traffic, it is unlikely that the town will ever again regain its former eminence. Nevertheless, it still retains its regional classification. Campbeltown whiskies are generally accepted to be quite distinctive, with a character which is mellower than that of the Islay malts, with a smoothness and a variable peatiness in the flavour.

ISLAY

Islay malts must be, for everyone from the beginner to the connoisseur, the most distinctive of all single malt whiskies – certainly, their flavour is among the strongest of all the regions. Peat is the key, both in terms of its influence on the ingredients used for distillation and of its presence in the final taste. The island has extensive beds of peat, over which the water used in the distillation process flows, arriving at its destination already flavoured. Varying amounts of peat are also used to dry the barley. In the past this latter ingredient, too, was produced locally, although now it may be brought in. Peat is noticeable in the flavours of all the Islay malts, from the mildest to the most intensely flavoured, imparting a dryness which is sometimes balanced by sweetness, sometimes emphasized by smokiness. For beginners to single malts, the Islay whiskies seem like an acquired taste, but they are an essential ingredient in the whisky-blending process, and the chances are that what you may think of as the distinctively Scottish flavour in your whisky is imparted by their presence in a blend.

HIGHLAND

Finally, the largest region, with more distilleries than the rest of the country combined, is Highland, probably the quintessential Scottish whisky production area. This is the land which lies to the north of the Highland line and includes distilleries as far apart as Inchmurrin in Dunbartonshire, Oban in Argyll, Pulteney in Wick and Highland Park in Orkney. As might be expected across such a wide area, generalizations become less valid and sub-division becomes more necessary. Geographical divisions of north, south, east and west, together with a special ones for Speyside and the islands, can be useful in illustrating particular characteristics.

North, South, East and West Highlands

The north Highland malts can be said to stretch from the area around Inverness up the east coast to Wick. The whiskies from this area are generally smooth, and while ranging from dry to fruity sweet, are not normally quite as peaty as some of their more southerly neighbours. Whisky from the southern Highlands – generally speaking, around the Perthshire area and to the west – is, as might be expected, softer and lighter in character, often reasonably sweet but with one or two dry examples. The western Highlands is the smallest of the Highland sub-divisions, encompassing the area from Oban to Fort William with their smooth, rounded whiskies. The eastern Highlands has distilleries spread out along the North Sea coast from Brechin in the south to Banff in the north. The whiskies in this area offer a wide range of styles, one of the widest of any of the sub-divisions, from fruity sweetness to peaty dryness.

Speyside

The largest and most famous of the Highland sub-divisions is that of Speyside, producing a range of single malts whose names are instantly recognizable, even to non-whisky drinkers: Macallan, Glenfiddich, Glenfarclas and Glenlivet. The area is concentrated around the Elgin–Dufftown district, a picturesque and fertile area whose remoteness made it an ideal location for the whisky smugglers of past centuries to escape the efforts of the excisemen.

REGIONAL CHARACTERISTICS

Speyside whiskies are recognized as being mellow, with a malty sweetness and light notes of peat: beyond this basic generalization, however, lies a wealth of variety and subtlety, and the Speyside malts can range from the aromatic and flowery to the robust and sherried. Whiskies can be found in this area to satisfy all palates, from the novice to the connoisseur, and for all occasions.

Island

The final Highland sub-group is that of the Island whiskies. As might be expected when these are viewed on a map, the classification is not so much based on characteristics as convenience – this is a suitable sub-group in which to deal with the remaining whiskies which do not fit in any other.

At present, the islands concerned are Jura, Mull and Skye in the west, and Orkney in the north. (It does not, of course, include Islay, whose distinctive style merits a category of its own.) However, in 1995 the Isle of Arran was added to this list with the opening of the first legal distillery on the island for 160 years at Lochranza; the single malt produced here should be available early in the new century. Once again, generalizations are difficult to make, with characters ranging from reasonably dry to full, sweet and malty.

As with any classification, these listings should not be taken as hard and fast rules – taste and preferences vary so greatly that they can only be general guidelines. The best way to decide how well particular whiskies fit their supposed regional listing or characteristic is simply to try each one for yourself!

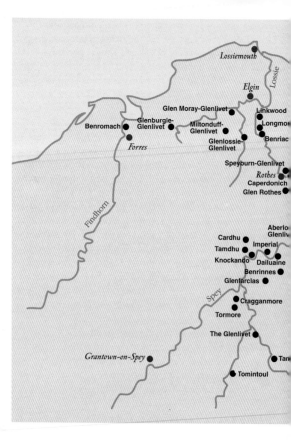

Lossiemouth

Elgin

Lossie

Glen Moray-Glenlivet
Linkwood

Benromach
Glenburgie-Glenlivet
Miltonduff-Glenlivet
Longmor

Benriac

Forres
Glenlossie-Glenlivet

Speyburn-Glenlivet

Rothes

Findhorn
Caperdonich

Glen Rothes

Aberlo
Glenliv

Cardhu
Imperial

Tamdhu

Knockando
Dailuaine

Benrinnes

Glenfarclas

Spey
Cragganmore

Tormore

The Glenlivet

Grantown-on-Spey
Tan

Tomintoul

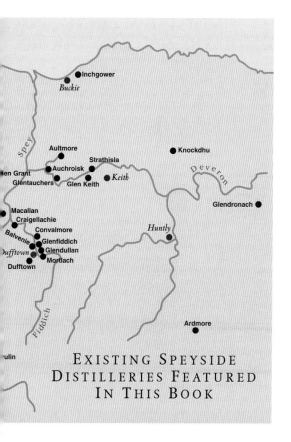

Inchgower
Buckie

Spey

Aultmore
Glen Grant
Glentauchers
Auchroisk
Strathisla
Glen Keith
Keith

Knockdhu

Deveron

Glendronach

Macallan
Craigellachie
Balvenie
Convalmore
Glenfiddich
Dufftown
Glendullan
Mortlach
Dufftown

Huntly

Ardmore

ulin

Fiddich

EXISTING SPEYSIDE
DISTILLERIES FEATURED
IN THIS BOOK

VISITING SCOTCH DISTILLERIES AND PRODUCERS

With more than 250,000 people visiting Scotland's distilleries every year, catering for visitors has become an important means of promotion and source of revenue for the more famous whisky-makers. Many distilleries are happy to accept visitors, and facilities range from a friendly, impromptu guided tour to a high-tech reception centre with organized tour and gift shop.

Glenmorangie Distillery in Tain, Ross-shire

The Pagoda Room Restaurant, part of the award-winning Glenturret visitor centre at Crieff in Perthshire (Glenturret Distillery Ltd)

Once you have decided which distilleries you would like to visit, you can telephone in advance to find out the particular facilities they offer – the telephone numbers of those distilleries which are equipped to receive visitors are given under their entries throughout the book. It is particularly advisable to telephone if you plan to visit during July and August. Although this is the height of the tourist season, it is also the traditional 'silent' period for this industry which was so closely associated with farming: closing the distillery at this time meant that the workers could help to gather in the harvest. The Scotch Whisky Association (tel: [Edinburgh] 0131-229 4383; [London] 0171-629 4384) publishes a useful leaflet detailing over forty distilleries which welcome visitors, together with opening times and booking information. The Scotch Whisky Heritage Centre (tel: 0131-220 0441) and the Scottish Tourist Board (head office, tel: 0131-332 2433) are also useful sources of information.

If you are in Edinburgh, a visit to the Scotch Whisky Heritage Centre on Castlehill is always a good starting point if you want to find out more about the industry, with exhibits which are both fun and educational. You can travel back through the industry's past, including the days of illicit distillation, viewing all from the comfort of your own motorized whisky cask!

Finally, for the opportunity to see a perfectly preserved traditional distillery, Dallas Dhu at Forres should not be missed if you are travelling through the north east. Established at the end of the nineteenth century, it stands in lovely countryside to the south of the town. It was previously owned by the Distillers Company, who closed it in 1983, and is now operated by the Historic Buildings and Monuments Commission for Scotland. Although it no longer produces whisky, it offers one of the most interesting distillery visits in Scotland. (Visitors are welcome 1000-1900 1 Apr.–30 Sept. Tel: 01309-72802 for details.)

PROFESSIONAL BODIES, MERCHANTS AND TRADE ASSOCIATIONS

As explained on pp. 35–36, single malts bottled by the distilleries are generally a marrying of casks from several distillations, with water being added to reduce the whisky to an agreed alcohol by volume strength for bottling. The whisky will also generally undergo a process of cold-temperature filtration to remove the residues which naturally precipitate cloudiness in the drink after dilution, when it is kept at low temperatures, or when it has ice added. Views differ as to whether this alters the character and taste of the whisky: the producers cite scientific evidence to show that there is no alteration to the whisky's character if it is not diluted below 40% alcohol by volume. However, various independent bodies believe that it does, and they offer consumers the chance to test for themselves.

The Scotch Malt Whisky Society (tel: 0131-554 3452) is one of these bodies. It buys from the distilleries selected single malts which it bottles straight from the cask and offers to its members, of whom there are over 18,000 around the world. The society aims to promote the increased understanding, appreciation and discerning consumption of malt whisky and has recently begun day-long whisky schools comprising practicals, lectures and tastings.

The independent spirit merchants, *William Cadenhead Ltd* (tel: 01586-554258), also subscribe to this view of the chill-filtration process, and pride themselves on maintaining the individuality of each batch of whisky, bottling straight from the cask at cask strength. The company's approach, of minimal interference with the whisky, relatively simple packaging, and the taking of care over content rather than presentation, is designed to appeal to the slightly more experienced whisky drinker. Much of Cadenhead's stock comes from distilleries whose produce is not otherwise available to the public.

Gordon and MacPhail of Elgin (tel: 01343-545111) also offer a wide range of their own bottlings from many distilleries. The company, owned and run by the Urquhart family, was established in 1895 as a wine and spirit merchant and licensed grocers, and now is regarded as the world's leading malt whisky specialists. Gordon and MacPhail's policy has always been to buy new whisky direct from a distillery, often in their own casks, warehousing it themselves and bottling it when they consider it to be at its best. Each barrel is assessed for quality, style and quantity available prior to bottling, thereby achieving a consistency and quality of malt for which the company is recognized. As well as single and vatted malts, cask-strength bottlings and unusual blends, they have a large selection of old and rare whiskies.

A relative newcomer to the independent merchants' ranks is the *Signatory Vintage Scotch Whisky Company*, based in Edinburgh (tel: 0131-555 4988). Founded in the late 1980s, they acquire casks of exceptional age and quality and bottle either diluted to 40%, 43% or 46%, or at cask strength. No colourant is used in their bottlings and only the diluted range is chill-filtered to remove oiliness. There is a variation between bottlings as the number of casks vatted varies.

For those whose interest is in the packaging as much as the contents, the *Mini Bottle Club* is the world's premier club for collectors of miniatures. Details can be obtained from the membership secretary, c/o 47 Burradon Rd, Burradon, Northumberland NE23 7NF (enclose a s.a.e.). A lisingt of those whiskies featured in this book which are available in miniature form is given on p.235.

Finally, if you would like to know more about any aspect of Scotch whisky, *The Scotch Whisky Association* will happily supply information for you. The association promotes the interests of the Scotch whisky industry in Britain and around the world, and its membership comprises almost all companies involved in the industry. The Public Affairs office is in London (tel: 0171-629 4384), while the head office is in Edinburgh (tel: 0131-229 4383).

READING THE LABEL

The label on a whisky bottle will allow you to identify a few basic facts about its contents even before you open the bottle – most obviously, the brand and its producers, the type of whisky it is, and its age, quantity and strength. Single malts normally proclaim themselves as such, and the identification of the producing distillery acts as a double check. A label which states a bottle's contents to be malt, but without the words 'single' or 'unblended', is probably vatted. Grains and blends likewise will identify themselves, and while most de luxe whiskies will also do so, this is not always the case. Blends of all kinds will carry the name of the blenders rather than of any distillery.

Where whiskies carry an age statement on the label, this will be the age of the youngest whisky in the bottle. Instead of this, some malts may give the year of their distillation. Single malts are usually eight years old and upwards, becoming more expensive as their age increases. It is generally held, however, that up to fifteen years is a good maturation period for whisky, and while some whiskies improve by maturing beyond this period, not all do of necessity – it depends on the individual whisky. Whiskies for general consumption in the UK are normally packaged in 70 or 75 cl bottles, but you may also come upon 1 litre bottles.

Most whiskies are sold at 40% alcohol by volume. The system for measuring spirit strength in Britain changed in 1980 from the older and more complicated Sikes system of measuring proof

brand name

age of whisky

type of whisky

strength (% alcohol by volume)

bottle volume

distiller

SPRINGBANK

ESTD 1828

AGED 30 YEARS

CAMPBELTOWN

Scotch SINGLE MALT Whisky

PRODUCT OF SCOTLAND

750ml Distilled by J. & A. MITCHELL & CO. LTD. 46% alc/vol
Springbank Distillery · Campbeltown · Scotland

The component parts of a single malt whisky label

strength, to the Organization of Legal Metrology, or OIML system, which measures spirit strength as a percentage of volume at 20 °C. Whisky is distilled at a much higher content than its final form for consumption. Water may be added before it goes into the cask, to bring it down to 68.5 % alcohol by volume, a standard measure. Some evaporation takes place as the whisky matures, leaving a final cask strength of around 45–60 %. Cask-strength whiskies are available, but most single malts have to have water added to bring them down to 40 % or 43 % (normally for the export market) strength for bottling. However, the industry may move towards a standard strength of 40% after a 1988 European Community directive which based the amount of duty on the alcoholic strength of a spirit. 40% alcohol by volume is equivalent to the old measure of 70° proof and, confusingly, 80° proof in the USA, which uses a slightly different system again.

READING THE LABEL

DEVELOPING THE PALATE
BY UNA HOLDEN-COSGROVE

Apart from the anatomical meaning – the roof of the mouth – a palate refers to the sense of taste, but the roof of the mouth does play an important role in discerning a taste. Spicy, hot and cold, pleasant and objectionable sensations are all in the province of the palate. Everyone has a different reaction to taste and both physically and psychologically the sense of smell has a major influence on how these sensations are perceived.

Where whisky is concerned, a palate needs to be educated in the same way as it must gradually be introduced to the different foods encountered in different countries – after all, a vindaloo is hardly the best introduction to curries! Similarly, a dram of one whisky can never be regarded as a real experience or a satisfacto-

ry introduction to the elixir of life. Every whisky has a different taste and smell: some are quite fierce, or vigorous, and others more honeyed and enticing. To attempt one of the more powerful malts, such as The Glenlivet or Talisker, without any previous knowledge of whisky can only kill any interest in proceeding further.

Unfortunately the early writers on whisky overlooked the fact that their palates were accustomed to the differing tastes and had been conditioned so that the robust types were more to their particular liking. As a result the malts and blends they recommended so highly were usually too powerful for the beginner, leading to an undeservedly macho image for malt whisky which meant that these stronger whiskies were more commonly found on the shelves of bars outside Scotland.

An ideal way to demonstrate this difference in taste is used at whisky-tasting sessions, where the participants are gently guided through a series of malts, starting with the softer, fruity smelling ones and slowly working through to the stronger ones. With this manipulation of the palate, almost invariably the participants find the final dram the most appealing! As these participants do not always appreciate that the aim of tastings is to show how good even the stronger malts are when the palate has been tutored, they are liable to seek out the strongest one to try again at a later date, only to find it tastes too strong – their palate has not really developed sufficiently to cope with it without more experience. So how should a palate be developed?

It is perhaps advisable to start with a whisky mix, as long as the whisky is a blend, or a grain such as Invergordon, and not a malt. Lemonade, soda, even water and ice are possible mixes for blended whisky. This will begin to train the senses and on cold days a Whisky Mac (blended whisky and Green Ginger) will provide a feeling of warmth that goes hand in hand with other pleasant sensations. A really fine blend – such as Black Bottle – can then be attempted neat.

Graduation to a malt requires good company and careful thought. For most beginners the spirit should not assail the taste buds, but inveigle the senses through an appealing scent, subtle taste and soothing after-effects. The aroma, which should be savoured before a sip is taken, can be spicy, fruity, flowery or peaty, and as with other scents like perfume and aftershave, individual preferences must be considered. The taste for the inexperienced should not be fierce – instead, the malt should be chosen from among the smooth, velvety and honeyed selections. Some are dry and others a little sweet, and once again personal preference must be recognized.

After-effects are every bit as important, as the palate can be attacked some time after a stronger malt has been imbibed, and this can be unpleasant to the unwary. There are a variety of exciting after-effects that should be experienced and appreciated. The sparkles on the tongue and roof of the mouth provided by such malts as Oban and Aberlour are quite delightful, the feeling of being massaged, not just in the mouth but all over the shoulders and back, as produced by such as Glendullan after only one sip will help to cure most stress reactions. There are sensations of glowing warmth in the mouth, further reminiscent tastes of fruit or other pleasant foods and even a very delayed sharpness that comes as an unexpected surprise.

The use of miniatures is extremely helpful in identifying whiskies that appeal most to an individual. Further tutoring of the palate should be by experiencing the stronger ones in graduated steps, rather than by assaulting an unprepared and unsuspecting mouth!

Very simply, to drink a malt whisky properly, in order to obtain maximum enjoyment, it is necessary to consider the smell, taste and after-effects that would appeal to a particular individual. Time should be spent appreciating the aroma, taking only a small sip, letting it roll around the mouth before swallowing it and then awaiting the enjoyment of its after-effects. It is also well to remember that mood and the time of day as well as the weather conditions play a role in palate appeal. What may at the end of a horrible day seem like the most wonderful malt on earth, could well appear boring and inadequate on a cold winter's night or overwhelming in the middle of a happy gathering on a glorious summer's afternoon. Remember, too, that a palate will change with experience.

There are many, many blends, a few grain whiskies, a number of vatted malts and about 160 single malts (from approximately 100 or so distilleries, with some producing more than one year and volume) from which to choose. All are different, each with a different effect on different palates and providing the customer with a wonderful choice and opportunity to learn about a fascinating topic. If the beginner treats whisky with respect, the experiences encountered in the process of development will prove enchanting.

The
Whiskies
of
Scotland

TASTE RATING

The discussions on the different whiskies which follow contain a taste rating of 1–5. This is not intended to be a judgement on the quality or relative standard of the spirit, nor is it possible to place strength and flavour together satisfactorily. Rather, it can be used as an indicator of accessibility of the whisky for a relatively inexperienced palate. A whisky may be mild or strong and still either lack flavour or exude it, so this rating concerns the degree of flavour, while at the same time allowing for the strength interfering with a person's ability to appreciate the flavour. The basic categories are as follows:

1	Popular with particular palates; spirituous, with a very mild flavour
2	Good for beginners; appealing taste and flavour for most palates at certain times
2–3	Also good for beginners, but a little stronger than 2. One to return to again and again
3	A dram for everyone; not too powerful, with pleasant sensations
3–4	This should also appeal to most tastes, but is slightly stronger, so the palate requires a little more experience
4	Very pleasing; a stronger spirit, ideal for those with more experience
5	Robust; only for the well developed palate

ABERFELDY

Aberfeldy Distillery, Aberfeldy, Perthshire

• AGE •
15 years

• STRENGTH •
43%

• TASTE RATING •
3

• COMMENTS •

Basically a dry malt with a medium body and clean, fresh character, but with a distinctly peaty background.

• VISITORS •

Visitors are welcome 0930–1630 Mon.–Fri. (times are restricted in winter). Telephone 01887-820330.

A berfeldy Distillery stands near the River Tay, at the town from which it takes its name. Building began in 1896 and the distillery opened two years later. It was built by Dewar but passed with that company into the ownership of the Distillers Company Ltd in 1925. Almost all of its production now goes into United Distillers' blends, most notably Dewar's White Label. The single malt is still relatively rare, only becoming available in official bottlings in the Distillery (Flora and Fauna) Malts series early in the 1990s.

ABERLOUR

**Aberlour-Glenlivet Distillery,
Aberlour, Banffshire**

• AGE •

10, 12, 15 years

• STRENGTH •

40%, 43%

• TASTE RATING •

3

• COMMENTS •

*A smooth, rich, sherried
Speyside malt which is an
ideal after-dinner drink.*

• VISITORS •

*Visitors are welcome by
appointment.*

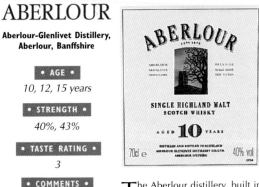

The Aberlour distillery, built in 1879, sits below Ben Rinnes from whose slopes it draws its water. In the distillery grounds is the well of St Drostan (or Dunstan), the tenth-century missionary and patron saint of Aberlour who later became Archbishop of Canterbury. Aquired by the Pernod Ricard company in 1974, Aberlour has been well-marketed in France, the U.K. and the U.S.A. where it is one of the most popular of Scotch whiskies. The company also owns the Irish Distillers Group.

AN CNOC

**Knockdhu Distillery,
Knock, Banffshire**

• AGE •

12 years

• STRENGTH •

40%

• TASTE RATING •

2-3

• COMMENTS •

An Cnoc's dryish aroma is complemented by a mellow sweetness in the flavour. This Highland malt was previously known as Knockdhu.

• VISITORS •

The distillery is not open to visitors.

Knockdhu Distillery was established in 1893 on a favoured site: with water available from Knock Hill, barley from the nearby farmlands, and a good supply of local peat. Although both its buildings and machinery have since been modified, the production process remains essentially the same, with the two originally designed pot stills remaining. In 1988, Knockdhu was sold to Inver House Distillers, who reopened it after a lengthy silent period.

SINGLE MALT

THE ANTIQUARY

United Distillers, Kilmarnock, Ayrshire

A smooth, well-balanced premium blend which displays the mellowness expected from its blend of whiskies all aged 12 years and over.

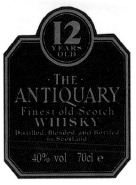

Now owned by United Distillers, Sanderson is the producer of The Antiquary. The company was one of the blenders who began trading in the early-to-mid nineteenth century and who were responsible for the popularizing of blended whiskies in the lucrative markets of southern England. William Sanderson was also a founder of the North British Distillery company in 1885 which ensured supplies of good grain whisky for his blends.

ARDBEG

**Ardbeg Distillery,
Port Ellen, Islay, Argyll**

• AGE •

17 years, 1978 vintage

• STRENGTH •

varies

• TASTE RATING •

5

• COMMENTS •

With a dominant peaty aroma and salty, orangey overtones, Ardbeg's insistently smoky flavour is balanced by sweeter notes. Ardbeg is considered one of the finest Islay malts.

• VISITORS •

Visitors are welcome at the distillery.

This distillery was opened in 1815, and was one of several established near the sea in an area originally used by smugglers. Nearby Lochs Uigeadale and Arinambeast supply the water which, together with local peat, produces a distinctively Islay malt. While under Allied Distillers ownership, the single malt was not officially produced and was only available from independent bottlers. After its purchase in 1997 by Glenmorangie plc, the distillery was restored and the single malt relaunched as a distillery bottling.

ARDMORE

**Ardmore Distillery,
Kennethmont,
Aberdeenshire**

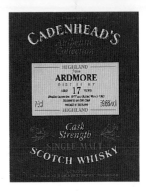

• AGE •
varies

• STRENGTH •
varies

• TASTE RATING •
4

• COMMENTS •

*A full-bodied Speyside malt
which is both robust and
sweet. An ideal after-dinner
dram, although it is not easy to
come by; available as a single
malt only through independent bottlers.*

• VISITORS •

*Visitors are welcome by
appointment. Telephone
01464-3213 to arrange.*

The distillery at Ardmore was built
in 1898 by the Teacher family of
whisky merchants and blenders.
Since that time almost all its production has gone into Teacher's
blends, most famously Highland
Cream. Today it is operated by Allied
Distillers, so its product also features
prominently in Allied's other blends.
Although the distillery has been
modernized it still retains some of
the original equipment, such as coal-fired stills, which were used in the
production of whisky at the end of
the nineteenth century.

AUCHENTOSHAN

**Auchentoshan Distillery,
Dalmuir, Dunbartonshire**

• AGE •

10, 21, 22, 25 years

• STRENGTH •

40% ,43%

• TASTE RATING •

2-3

• COMMENTS •

A light, sweetish whisky whose smooth qualities are perhaps partially owed to the process of triple, rather than the more common double distillation.

• VISITORS •

The distillery is not open to visitors.

Although Auchentoshan Distillery lies south of the Highland Line, it uses water from north of the line, so theoretically could be said to have a foot in both camps. It is, however, officially recognized as a Lowland distillery and whisky. Founded in the early nineteenth century, part of its interesting history includes surviving bombing in the Clydebank Blitz during the Second World War, when a stream of blazing whisky was said to have flowed from the building. It is presently owned by Morrison Bowmore.

SINGLE MALT

AULTMORE

**Aultmore Distillery,
Aultmore, Keith, Banffshire**

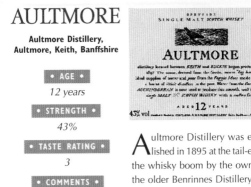

SPEYSIDE
SINGLE MALT *SCOTCH* WHISKY

AULTMORE

distillery located between KEITH and BUCKIE began production in 1897. The name, derived from the Gaelic, means "big burn". Ideal supplies of water and peat from the Foggie Moss made this area a haven of illicit distillers in the past. Water from the flows of AUCHINDERRAN is now used to produce this smooth, well balanced single MALT SCOTCH WHISKY with a curious finish.

AGED 12 YEARS

43% vol .... SCOTLAND. A.A.MORE DISTILLERY ...... 70 cl

- **AGE**

12 years

- **STRENGTH**

43%

- **TASTE RATING**

3

- **COMMENTS**

*A faintly peaty aroma leads
into this smooth, fruity, well-
balanced whisky which has
become – deservedly – better
known in recent years.*

- **VISITORS**

The distillery is open to visitors
by appointment only.
Telephone 01542-882762 to
arrange.

Aultmore Distillery was established in 1895 at the tail-end of
the whisky boom by the owner of
the older Benrinnes Distillery. The
area, with its abundant peat and
water supplies, was infamous in the
past for illicit distilling. Peat used in
the production process is taken from
a nearby moss, and the water is
taken from local springs. The
distillery passed to Dewars in 1923,
and was improved and upgraded in
the 1970s. It is now owned by
United Distillers who have been
officially bottling its single malt in
their Distillery (Flora and Fauna)
Malts series since the early 1990s.

THE BAILIE NICOL JARVIE

MacDonald and Muir, Leith, Edinburgh

• AGE •

12 years minimum

• STRENGTH •

40%

• TASTE RATING •

2

• COMMENTS •

A light, subtle whisky with a sweet, well-balanced aroma and a smooth, lingering finish.

Founded in 1893 in Leith by Roderick Macdonald and Alexander Muir, Macdonald and Muir Ltd is one of the few remaining independent family-owned and controlled companies left in the Scotch whisky trade. 'The Bailie', or 'BNJ' as it is also known, is named after the fictional magistrate in Walter Scott's *Rob Roy*. Although a popular brand in the early years of this century (particularly in military circles), in recent years production had been severely limited. However, the brand was relaunched in October 1994 and production stepped up following a change in the blend receipe.

BALBLAIR

**Balblair Distillery,
Edderton, Tain, Ross-shire**

• AGE •

10 years

• STRENGTH •

40%

• TASTE RATING •

3

• COMMENTS •

*A distinctive Highland malt
whose slightly dry sharpness
is nicely balanced by a light
note of sweetness. Good as an
aperitif, it is available only
from independent bottlers.*

• VISITORS •

*The distillery is not open to
visitors.*

Although its origins are lost in the
mists of illicit distillation, it is
claimed that Balblair was founded
in 1749, which would make it one of
the oldest distilleries in the country.
The present buildings, dating from
the 1870s, are set in pretty countryside in an area known as the 'parish
of peats'. The distillery had very
recently been mothballed by its then
owners, Allied Distillers, but was
acquired from them in the spring of
1996 by the independent Inver
House Distillers. The addition of
Balblair gives Inver House four malt
distilleries – Knockdhu, Speyburn-
Glenlivet and Pultney.

SINGLE MALT

BALLANTINE'S FINEST

**Allied Distillers,
Dumbarton, Dunbartonshire**

STRENGTH

40%, 43%

TASTE RATING

2-3

COMMENTS

Ballantine's Finest is, like Allied Distillers' other blends, characteristically mellow and well-rounded with a soft, un-assertive peaty flavour.

VISITORS

The plant is not suitable for visitors.

Ballantine's was bought in 1936 by Hiram Walker as one of their first moves into the Scotch whisky market. Glenburgie and Miltonduff distilleries followed in 1937 and their new, giant complex in Dumbarton, featuring grain and malt distilleries, was operational the following year. Today the group is owned by Allied Domecq and operated by their wholly Scottish-based subsidiary, Allied Distillers. The Dumbarton plant is renowned locally for its 'Scotchwatch' alarm system, comprising 100-odd noisy Chinese geese!

BALMENACH

**Balmenach Distillery,
Cromdale, Moray**

- **AGE** -

12 years

- **STRENGTH** -

43%

- **TASTE RATING** -

4

- **COMMENTS** -

*A complicated, full-bodied
malt best suited as an after-
dinner dram. It is still relatively
rare, only becoming available
in official bottlings in the
Distillery (Flora and Fauna)
Malts series early in the 1990s.*

The Balmenach Distillery, in the
Haughs of Cromdale, is set in an
area which was notorious for illicit
distilling for many years before the
Licensing Act of 1823. Built in 1824
by James McGregor (great-grandfa-
ther of Sir Robert Bruce Lockhart,
author of the classic 1951 book,
Scotch), Balmenach was one of the
first distilleries in the Highlands to
be licensed under the 1823 act. The
distillery was acquired by United
Distillers and most of its production
went into the company's blends but
has since been closed.

ESTD 1892

SINGLE MALT

Distilled at

THE BALVENIE

Distillery, Banffshire

SCOTLAND

SINGLE BARREL

MALT SCOTCH WHISKY

from a single barrel

AGED 15 YEARS

BOTTLED BY HAND

70cle   PRODUCT OF SCOTLAND   50.4%vol

THE BALVENIE

**Balvenie Distillery,
Dufftown, Keith, Banffshire**

• AGE •

10 years (Founder's Reserve),
12 years (Doublewood),
15 years (Single Barrel)

• STRENGTH •

varies

• TASTE RATING •

3-4

• COMMENTS •

Founder's Reserve has a rich
colour, bouquet and flavour
with a smooth, clean, dry
finish. Doublewood is full-
bodied, yet smooth and
mellow, and Single Barrel, a
harder-to-obtain 15-year-old,
is a single-cask bottling.

• VISITORS •

The distillery is not open to
visitors.

B uilt in 1892 near the ruins of
fourteenth-century Balvenie
Castle by the Grants of Glenfiddich,
Balvenie Distillery has now been
owned by an independent family
company for five generations.
Balvenie Distillery still grows its own
barley, malts in its own traditional
floor maltings, employs coopers to
tend the barrels and coppersmiths
to tend the stills. The Balvenie is
most unusual in producing a range
of three malt whiskies of different
age and character.

BANFF

**Banff Distillery,
Banff, Banffshire**

- **AGE**

varies

- **STRENGTH**

varies

- **TASTE RATING**

2–3

- **COMMENTS**

*A pleasant, slightly smoky,
sweet bouquet leads into a
whisky with a rather assertive
taste. A rare malt, it is available from independent
merchants only.*

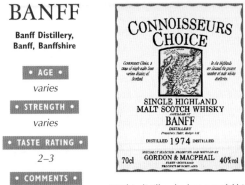

This distillery had an eventful history after its founding in 1863. It
survived damage by fire in the
1870s, and was one of the few distilleries to be bombed during the
Second World War, when thousands
of gallons of whisky had to be
thrown away to prevent the spread of
fire. The distillery also once supplied
whisky to Parliament. It was closed
down by its parent company, the
Distillers Company Ltd, in 1983, and
has since been demolished.

BELL'S EXTRA SPECIAL

United Distillers, Glasgow

• STRENGTH •

40%

• TASTE RATING •

2-3

• COMMENTS •

The most popular blend in the UK, Bell's Extra Special is a pleasant, medium-bodied whisky with a nutty aroma and a spicy flavour.

The merchants and blending company which ultimately became Arthur Bell & Sons was begun in Perth in 1825. Bell himself joined the firm in the 1840s and became a partner in 1851. The 'Extra Special' name, accompanied by Bell's signature, was registered as a trade mark in 1895 and large-scale expansion came in the 1930s after the ending of Prohibition in the USA. Bell's is now owned by United Distillers who relaunched Bell's Extra Special as an 8-year-old blend in 1994.

BLEND

BEN NEVIS

**Ben Nevis Distillery,
Fort William, Inverness-shire**

- **AGE**

10, 19, 25, 26 years

- **STRENGTH**

varies

- **TASTE RATING**

3

- **COMMENTS**

*Ranging from pale amber to a
deep, golden colour, Ben
Nevis is characterized by its
fresh, slightly peaty flavour
and smooth finish.*

- **VISITORS**

*Visitors are welcome
0900–1700 Mon.–Fri. all year
(0900–1730 Jul.–Aug.) and
1000–1600 Sat., Easter–Sep.
Larger parties are advised to
telephone 01397-700200 to
arrange.*

B en Nevis Distillery, standing at
the foot of Scotland's highest
mountain, is one of the oldest
distilleries in Scotland. It was
founded at Fort William by the
famous local character, 'Long'
John Macdonald in 1825. (The brand
name of Long John and the distillery
company became separated.) After
more than 100 years in the family,
the distillery was sold in 1941. The
subsequent addition of a patent still
made the distillery one of the few
that could produce both malt and
grain under one roof, and it received
a new lease of life in the 1980s
following its acquisition by the Nikka
Whisky Distilling Co. of Japan.

BENRIACH DISTILLERY
EST. 1898
A S I N G L E
PURE HIGHLAND MALT
Scotch Whisky
Benriach Distillery, in the heart of the Highlands,
still malts its own barley. The resulting whisky has
a unique and attractive delicacy
PRODUCED AND BOTTLED BY THE
BENRIACH
DISTILLERY C?
ELGIN, MORAYSHIRE, SCOTLAND, IV30 3SJ
Distilled and Bottled in Scotland
AGED 10 YEARS
70 cl e 43%vol

BENRIACH

**Benriach Distillery,
Longmorn, near Elgin, Moray**

• AGE •

10 years

• STRENGTH •

43%

• TASTE RATING •

4

• COMMENTS •

A medium-bodied, fruity whisky with sweetish overtones and a gently malty finish. A new bottling has been available from the distillery since 1994.

• VISITORS •

Visitors are welcome by appointment.

Originally built in 1898, Benriach was closed in 1900, after recession hit the previously booming whisky industry. It was refitted and reopened in 1965, although not completely modernized, still retaining its hand-turned malting floor. Benriach is in fact one of the few distilleries in Scotland still malting barley on the premises in the traditional manner. The company has been owned by Seagram since 1978, and most of its produce goes into their blends. across.

BENRINNES

**Benrinnes Distillery,
Aberlour, Banffshire**

* AGE *

15 years

* STRENGTH *

43%

* TASTE RATING *

4

* COMMENTS *

*This is a complex Speyside
malt which has hints of wood
and grass to its flavour, and a
fruity aftertaste.*

* VISITORS *

*The distillery is open to visitors by appointment only.
Telephone 01340-871215.*

Built almost 700 feet up the slopes of Ben Rinnes, from which it takes its name, this distillery is believed to have been founded in 1835 although evidence exists of distilling on this site in 1826. It was largely rebuilt and modernized in the 1950s. Most of its production is distilled three times rather than the more usual twice, and almost all is used in United Distillers' blends. The single malt is still relatively rare, only becoming available in official bottlings in the Distillery (Flora and Fauna) Malts series early in the 1990s.

BENROMACH

**Benromach Distillery,
Forres, Moray**

• AGE •

varies

• STRENGTH •

varies

• TASTE RATING •

2-3

• COMMENTS •

Subtle and sweet, this Speyside malt has a gentle, fragrant palate and refreshing aftertaste. It is available from independent merchants.

• VISITORS •

Visitors are welcome 0900–1700 Mon.–Fri. all year (0900–1730 Jul.– Aug.) and 1000–1600 Sat., Easter–Sept. Larger parties should telephone 01397-700200 to arrange.

Benromach was built just outside Forres in 1898, in the years of expansion for the whisky industry, and it underwent extensive reconstruction in 1966 and 1974. It passed through several hands until coming to rest with the Distillers Company Ltd in 1953. Supplies may not be easy to come by for the immediate future as the distillery was closed from 1983 to 1993, when it was sold by United Distillers to the independent merchants and bottlers Gordon and MacPhail. Since then it has been re-fitted, and new distillation began in 1996.

BIG "T"

**Tomatin Distillery Company,
Tomatin, Inverness-shire**

• AGE •

*5 years (standard blend)
12 years (de luxe)*

• STRENGTH •

40%, 43%

• TASTE RATING •

*1 (standard blend)
2 (de luxe)*

• COMMENTS •

Big "T" standard blend is a whisky of light-to-medium body with a fresh, malty sweetness, well-balanced by a hint of peat. The 12-year-old de luxe is an extremely smooth blend, most of which is reserved for export.

• VISITORS •

Visitors can visit the malt whisky distillery; see the entry on Tomatin for details.

FINEST SCOTCH WHISKY

BIG "T"

SCOTCH WHISKY

100% BLENDED SCOTCH WHISKIES
BLENDED AND BOTTLED
IN SCOTLAND BY
THE TOMATIN DISTILLERY COMPANY LTD.

TOMATIN SCOTLAND

43% Vol   75 cl

The Tomatin Distillery Company's premises is not only one of the highest in the country (at over 1000 feet up in the Monadhliath Mountains), it is also the largest-capacity distillery in the country, with production as high as five million gallons per annum. The company declined in the 1980s and went into receivership, but was bought by the Japanese firms of Takara Schuzo and Okura, thus becoming the first Scotch whisky distillery to be acquired by Japanese owners.

BLACK & WHITE

United Distillers, Banbeath, Leven, Fife

• STRENGTH •

40%

• TASTE RATING •

2

• COMMENTS •

A clean, pleasantly mild blend, Black & White has a fresh, grassy flavour, which is complemented by a light sweetness. Black & White is currently available only outside the UK.

Black & White is the standard blend of the company begun in 1884 by James Buchanan as a whisky blenders and merchants in London. It was an immediate success, with a contract to supply the House of Commons, and the firm was important in the introduction of blended whiskies to the English market. The whisky was originally bottled and labelled in a very distinctive black and white livery, and this popular nickname eventually was adopted as the brand name.

BLACK BOTTLE

**Matthew Gloag & Son,
Perth, Perthshire**

- STRENGTH -

40%

- TASTE RATING -

2–3

- COMMENTS -

*Black Bottle is a smooth,
superior-quality blend with a
fresh hint of peat, complemented by sweeter, malty
notes.*

- VISITORS -

*The plant is not suitable for
visitors.*

Black Bottle was first produced by a family of merchants from Aberdeen in 1879, and has been a premium blend ever since it first appeared on the market. The company was sold to Long John International in 1959, later being acquired by Allied Distillers in 1990, before ultimately passing into the control of Matthew Gloag, the producers of The Famous Grouse blend. A big seller in the Scottish market, Black Bottle is linked to Laphroaig. Its distinctive pot-still-shaped bottle, used almost since its first appearance, rapidly became its trademark and has remained virtually unchanged to the present day.

LOWLAND
SINGLE MALT
SCOTCH WHISKY

The *Broad Leaved Helleborine*,
a rare species of *wild orchid*, can be found growing
in the *ancient oak woodland* behind the

BLADNOCH

distillery. The most southerly in *SCOTLAND*,
founded in the early 1800's, *(5th)* the
distillery stands by the *RIVER BLADNOCH*
near *Wigtown*. It produces a *distinctly*
LOWLAND *single* MALT WHISKY – *delicate* and
fruity with a *lemony* aroma and *taste*.

A G E D **10** Y E A R S

43% vol   70 cl

BLADNOCH

**Bladnoch Distillery,
Bladnoch, Wigtown,
Wigtownshire**

• AGE •

10 years

• STRENGTH •

43%

• TASTE RATING •

3

• COMMENTS •

Bladnoch is a light-to-medium-bodied malt with a light, fragrant, lemony aroma and a gentle, unassertive flavour with fruity tones.

Bladnoch was Scotland's most southerly distillery, in Wigtownshire, and was also one of its oldest. It was built in 1817 and stood on the banks of the River Bladnoch, in the village of the same name. It had many owners throughout the course of the twentieth century, the latest being United Distillers. The distillery is now closed. Bladnoch's single malt is still relatively rare, only becoming available in official bottlings in UD's Distillery (Flora and Fauna) Malts series early in the 1990s.

BLAIR ATHOL

Blair Athol Distillery, Pitlochry, Perthshire

- **AGE**

  12 years

- **STRENGTH**

  43%

- **TASTE RATING**

  2–3

- **COMMENTS**

A light, fresh single malt with dry notes and a hint of smokiness.

- **VISITORS**

Visitors are welcome 0930–1700 Mon.-Sat. all year, and 1200–1700 Sun., Easter–October. Tele-phone 01796-472234 to arrange.

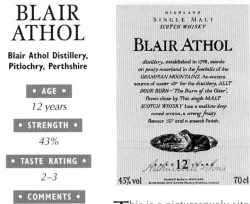

HIGHLAND
SINGLE MALT
SCOTCH WHISKY

BLAIR ATHOL

distillery, established in 1798, stands on *peaty moorland* in the *foothills* of the *GRAMPIAN MOUNTAINS*. An ancient source of *water* for the distillery, ALLT DOUR BURN – 'The Burn of the Otter', flows close by. This *single MALT SCOTCH WHISKY* has a *mellow deep toned* aroma, a *strong fruity* flavour and a *smooth* finish.

Aged **12** *Years*

Arthur Bell & Sons

43% vol   Distilled & Bottled in SCOTLAND
BLAIR ATHOL DISTILLERY, Pitlochry, Perthshire, Scotland   70 cl

This is a picturesquely sited distillery on a wooded hillside on the outskirts of the pretty Perthshire tourist centre of Pitlochry. Blair Athol is unusual in that it is twelve miles distant from the village after which it is named. Established in 1825, the distillery was bought by Bells in 1933 and sympathetically upgraded. It is now owned by United Distillers. Its water comes from the Allt Dour (Burn of the Otter) which flows past the distillery en route to the River Tummel.

BOWMORE

Bowmore Distillery, Bowmore, Islay, Argyll

• AGE •
12, 15, 17, 21, 22, 25, 30 years

• STRENGTH •
40%, 43%

• TASTE RATING •
3

• COMMENTS •
With its pleasant aroma and peaty–fruity flavour, Bowmore is a good Islay malt for newcomers to these distinctive whiskies to try.

• VISITORS •
Visitors are welcome by appointment. Telephone 01496-810671 to arrange.

Established in 1779, Bowmore is reputed to be the oldest legal distillery on Islay. It stands in the island's main town and overlooks Loch Indaal, and its water is taken from the peaty River Laggan. The distillery has passed through several hands in the twentieth century, but it has been a consistently thriving concern since its acquisition in 1963 by Stanley P. Morrison of Glasgow. The company is now Morrison Bowmore, and this is their flagship distillery.

SINGLE MALT

BRUICHLADDICH

**Bruichladdich Distillery,
Bruichladdich, Islay, Argyll**

• AGE •

*10, 15, 21, 15/21,
26 years*

• STRENGTH •

40%

• TASTE RATING •

3

• COMMENTS •

*A subtle malt, and less
medicinal in its flavour than
other Islay whiskies,
Bruichladdich is a lightish, dry,
fresh-tasting whisky.*

The
BRUICHLADDICH
ISLAY
Single *Malt*
SCOTCH • WHISKY

DISTILLED, MATURED AND BOTTLED BY
BRUICHLADDICH DISTILLERY COMPANY LIMITED
BRUICHLADDICH, ISLE OF ISLAY, SCOTLAND

AGED **10** YEARS

7Ocl   40%vol

Built in 1881, Bruichladdich is Scotland's most westerly distillery. Its water comes from an inland reservoir and, unlike the other distilleries, is not drawn from springs which have flowed over peaty land; this has been suggested as a reason why its peaty flavour is less intense than other Islay malts. Bruichladdich was owned by Invergordon Distillers from 1972 until 1993, but since the company's acquisition that year by Whyte & Mackay, it has been mothballed along with two of the group's other distilleries, Tamnavulin and Tullibardine.

BUNNAHABHAIN

**Bunnahabhain Distillery,
Port Askaig, Islay, Argyll**

• AGE •

12 years

• STRENGTH •

40%

• TASTE RATING •

3

• COMMENTS •

Less characteristically peaty than some other Islay malts, Bunnahabhain is a fresh, light and mellow whisky with a soft smooth flavour.

• VISITORS •

Visitors are welcome by appointment. Telephone 01496-840646 to arrange.

Bunnahabhain (which means 'mouth of the river', in reference to its location on the river Margadale) was founded in 1881 by the Greenlees brothers. They formed the Islay Distillery Company and bought Glen Rothes Distillery in 1887, which together formed the Highland Distilleries Company who still own Bunnahabhain today. The distillery was originally sited in an uninhabited, inhospitable part of the island but over the years a small hamlet has grown up around it.

CAMERON BRIG

**Cameronbridge Distillery,
Cameron Bridge, Fife**

● STRENGTH ●

40%

● TASTE RATING ●

1

● COMMENTS ●

*Like other grain whiskies, a
lighter spirit than malt, with a
fresh taste and an element of
smoothness.*

● VISITORS ●

*The distillery is not open to
visitors.*

Cameronbridge Distillery had
been operating for several years
before it was acquired in 1824 by
John Haig, one of the famous family
of Lowland whisky distillers. Haig's
company were among the founders
of the Distillers Company in 1877,
and United Distillers still own the
distillery today. Cameronbridge
produced both grain and malt
whisky using a mixture of pot and
patent stills until 1929 before finally
concentrating on grain alone.

CAOL ILA

Caol Ila Distillery, Port Askaig, Islay, Argyll

• AGE •

15 years

• STRENGTH •

43%

• TASTE RATING •

4

• COMMENTS •

Nicely balanced, Caol Ila is not the most peaty of the Islay whiskies, but is pleasantly dry with a well-rounded body.

• VISITORS •

Visitors are welcome Mon.–Fri. by appointment. Telephone 01496-840207 to arrange.

Caol Ila was established in 1846 and overlooks the Sound of Islay (which is also the English translation of its name). It previously used its own wharf for the despatching of its product. The distillery has been rebuilt twice, at almost 100-year intervals, in 1879 and 1972. The most recent modernization almost doubled the distillery's output. Caol Ila is now owned by United Distillers. The single malt is still relatively rare, only becoming available in official bottlings in UD's Distillery (Flora and Fauna) Malts series early in the 1990s.

CAPERDONICH

**Caperdonich Distillery,
Rothes, Moray**

• AGE •

varies

• STRENGTH •

varies

• TASTE RATING •

3

• COMMENTS •

A pleasant Speyside malt of light-to-medium body, with a delicately fruity flavour combined with a hint of peat. Used mostly for blending, it is only available from independent merchants.

• VISITORS •

The distillery is not open to visitors.

Originally owned by J & J Grant, this distillery was built across the road from their main production centre at Glen Grant. The two distilleries were to be treated as one for licensing purposes, so a pipe spanned the road to carry the produce of Caperdonich (then known as Glen Grant Number Two) across for blending. Built to take advantage of the boom years of the 1890s, it suffered with the fall-off in consumption and was closed in the early 1900s, waiting over sixty years for renovation and reopening under the new name of Caperdonich.

CARDHU

**Cardhu Distillery,
Knockando, Moray**

• AGE •

12 years

• STRENGTH •

40%

• TASTE RATING •

2-3

• COMMENTS •

*A smooth, light malt of silky
character and delicate, sweet
flavour which make it accessible to all from the novice to the
connoisseur.*

• VISITORS •

*Visitors are welcome
0930–1630 Mon.–Fri. all year,
and 0930–1630 Sat., May–
Sept. Tele-phone 01340-
810204.*

Whisky distilling had been carried on illegally in this area
for a long time before Cardow
Distillery, as it was then, was founded and licensed in 1824. The
distillery was bought by John Walker
of Kilmarnock during the boom
years of the 1890s, producing a vatted and a single malt under the
Cardhu name. It was modernized in
1965 and its single malt was
relaunched, with the distillery name
being changed in 1981 to match
that of its product. It is now owned
by United Distillers. Cardhu enjoys
a splendid situation and has recently been refurbished.

CHIVAS REGAL

Chivas Brothers, Paisley, Renfrewshire

• AGE •
12 years

• STRENGTH •
40%

• TASTE RATING •
2–3

• COMMENTS •

A classic de luxe blend with a malty sweetness and a trace of peatiness in its flavours.

Chivas Brothers is a subsidiary of the Canadian drinks firm Seagram, by whom it was bought in 1949. The origins of the Chivas Brothers company can be traced back to the establishment of a wine and spirit merchant and licensed grocer in Aberdeen in 1801. Owning nine malt distilleries, Seagram is an important company in the Scotch whisky market. Chivas Regal is one of several Seagram blends which include Passport, 100 Pipers and the premium 21-year-old Royal Salute.

THE CLAYMORE

Whyte & Mackay, Glasgow

• STRENGTH •

40%

• TASTE RATING •

2-3

• COMMENTS •

A nicely rounded, medium-bodied blend with a mellow aroma and a well-balanced, smooth and rich taste.

• VISITORS •

The blending and bottling plant is not open to visitors.

The Claymore is a popular blend owned by Whyte & Mackay, the blending and bottling company begun in 1882 by whisky merchants James Whyte and Charles Mackay. As with many of the company's whiskies, The Claymore is popular in export markets as well as in the UK, where it is among the best-selling blends. In 1993 Whyte & Mackay acquired Invergordon Distillers, adding seven malt distilleries and the big Invergordon grain distillery to their holdings.

CLYNELISH

Clynelish Distillery, Brora, Sutherland

- **AGE**

14 years

- **STRENGTH**

43%

- **TASTE RATING**

3

- **COMMENTS**

Clynelish is a medium-bodied, full-flavoured whisky with many devotees. It is slightly dry to the taste, with a hint of peat.

- **VISITORS**

Visitors are welcome 0930–1630 Mon.–Fri. Telephone 01408-621444.

The original distillery on this site was built in 1819 by the man who became the 1st Duke of Sutherland, the prime mover in the most infamous of the Highland Clearances. Its purpose was to make full use of the cheap grain grown on the new coastal farms of his newly-cleared tenants. A new distillery (now owned by United Distillers) was built on adjacent land in 1967–68, taking the name Clynelish, while the original distillery, renamed Brora, continued until 1983.

COLEBURN

**Coleburn Distillery,
Longmorn, Elgin, Moray**

• AGE •
varies

• STRENGTH •
varies

• TASTE RATING •
3

• COMMENTS •
A difficult-to-find malt with a delicate, fragrant aroma and pleasant, slightly flowery taste. Available bottled by independent merchants.

• VISITORS •
Visitors are welcome 0900–1700 Mon.–Fri. all year (0900–1730 Jul.– Aug.) and 1000–1600 Sat., Easter–Sept. Larger parties should telephone 01397-700200 to arrange.

Coleburn was built by John Robertson of Dundee in 1896 and was licensed to J. & G. Stewart, a subsidiary of the Distillers Company Ltd and blenders of Usher's whiskies. It was acquired by United Distillers and mothballed in 1985. Almost all of its produce went into blends, and since its closure, its malt has become even rarer.

COLUMBA CREAM

John Murray & Co (Mull), Calgary, Isle of Mull

• AGE •

4 years

• STRENGTH •

17%

• TASTE RATING •

2

• COMMENTS •

A blend of fine single malt whiskies, with the addition of honey and cream makes for a very pleasant and mellow whisky cream liqueur.

• VISITORS •

The plant is not open to visitors.

John Murray & Co. have been producing Columba Cream for several years to a formula which is based on a traditional recipe. With five single malts included in its recipe, this high-quality cream liqueur is an exceptionally fine example of its type. The company has offices on the Isle of Mull, and blending and bottling is currently carried out at their plant in Perth.

CONVALMORE

**Convalmore Distillery,
Dufftown, Keith, Banffshire**

**SINGLE SPEYSIDE
MALT SCOTCH WHISKY**
DISTILLED AT
CONVALMORE
DISTILLERY
Proprietors: W.P. Lowrie & Co. Ltd
DISTILLED **1969** DISTILLED
SPECIALLY SELECTED, PRODUCED AND BOTTLED BY
70cl **GORDON & MACPHAIL** 40%vol
ELGIN · SCOTLAND
PRODUCE OF SCOTLAND

• AGE •

varies

• STRENGTH •

varies

• TASTE RATING •

3

• COMMENTS •

*Almost all the production of
Convalmore goes into blends
and so is available as a single
malt only from independent
merchants. It is a dry, aromatic,
and atypical Speyside malt
which works best as a digestif.*

W.P. Lowrie, the present licensed distillers, bought Convalmore in 1904, eleven years after its founding. Considerably damaged by fire, it was rebuilt in 1910 when experiments were made in the production of malt whisky from patent stills; this was abandoned in 1916, however, in favour of the traditional pot-still method which was considered to mature the whisky better. It was acquired by United Distillers and was mothballed in 1985.

CRAGGANMORE

**Cragganmore Distillery,
Ballindalloch, Banffshire**

• AGE •
12 years

• STRENGTH •
40%

• TASTE RATING •
3–4

• COMMENTS •

*A Speyside malt of distinctive
and complex character,
Cragganmore has a delicate
aroma and smoky finish.*

• VISITORS •

*The distillery is not open to
visitors.*

Cragganmore was built in 1869 and was the first distillery to be constructed alongside an existing railway and so utilise the then new mode of transport for distribution. The distillery took its name from nearby Craggan More Hill. It was built by John Smith (a man of great bulk, also known locally as 'Cragganmore') and is now licensed to D. & J. McCallum. Most of its production goes into blends, especially Old Parr, and until a few years ago, the single malt was only infrequently available. The distillery is owned by United Distillers.

CRAIGELLACHIE

**Craigellachie Distillery,
Craigellachie, Aberlour,
Banffshire**

• AGE •

14 years

• STRENGTH •

43%

• TASTE RATING •

3

• COMMENTS •

A smoky-smelling and -tasting malt of medium body, Craigellachie works well as an after-dinner dram. It is generally available from independent whisky merchants.

• VISITORS •

The distillery is not open to visitors.

This distillery is pleasantly situated on high ground above the River Spey outside Dufftown. It was built in 1891 by the Craigellachie Distillery Co., a founder of which was Peter Mackie, the creator of the White Horse brand. Mackie and Co. (later White Horse Distillers) subsequently bought the distillery in 1915. It is now owned by United Distillers and most of its production is devoted to blending. The single malt is still relatively rare, only becoming available in official bottlings in the Distillery (Flora and Fauna) Malts series early in the 1990s.

CRAWFORD'S THREE STAR

Whyte & Mackay, Glasgow

* STRENGTH *

40%

* TASTE RATING *

2

* COMMENTS *

A smooth, nicely balanced blend with light, malty flavours. The de luxe Five Star is a richer whisky with mild sherried hints.

A & A. Crawford was established as a whisky merchant and blenders in Leith in 1860. Although the original founders died before the end of the century, the business was taken over by their sons who were responsible for the launching of the successful Crawford's Three Star blend at the start of the century. The de luxe Five Star appeared in the 1920s and was also well received. Acquired by the Distillers Company Ltd in 1944, ownership passed to Whyte & Mackay in 1986.

BLEND

CUTTY SARK

Berry Brothers & Rudd Ltd, London

A delicate, smooth whisky with a fresh, crisp taste. A high proportion of oak-matured Speyside malts contributes greatly to its smooth taste.

Berry Brothers & Rudd, London wine and spirit merchants since the seventeenth century, launched the Cutty Sark blend in 1923 specifically for the US market, where it quickly became a brand leader, a position it has sustained ever since. It is also a leading premium blend in countries such as Greece, Japan, Spain, Portugal, Korea and Brazil. It takes its name from the famous clipper ship built in Scotland in 1869, renowned as one of the fastest sailing ships of its day.

CUTTY SARK EMERALD

Berry Brothers & Rudd Ltd, London

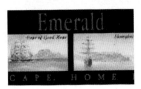

Cutty Sark Emerald has a soft, honeyed fruit aroma, a hint of sweetness on the palate and a rounded, lengthy finish.

Berry Brothers & Rudd have been successful London wine and spirit merchants since the seventeenth century. The original Cutty Sark blend was launched in 1923 specifically for the American market, where it quickly became a brand leader, a position it has sustained ever since. A blend of oak-matured whiskies of at least 12 years of age, Cutty Sark Emerald has strong international following, particularly in Japan, Korea, Portugal, Spain and Greece.

BLEND

CUTTY SARK GOLDEN JUBILEE

Berry Brothers & Rudd Ltd, London

Berry Brothers & Rudd have been successful London wine and spirit merchants since the seventeenth century. Cutty Sark Golden Jubilee is a commemoration of Queen Victoria's reign and the handsome gift-box packaging illustrates the achievements of that age. It is produced from Berry Bros & Rudd's own private whisky reserves and contains very fine rare whiskies, some over 50 years old. Golden Jubilee is available primarily in selected duty free outlets in Asia Pacific

DAILUAINE

**Dailuaine Distillery,
Carron, Banffshire**

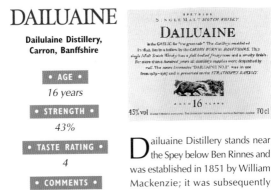

SPEYSIDE
SINGLE MALT SCOTCH WHISKY

DAILUAINE

in the GAELIC for "the green vale." The distillery, established in 1852, lies in a hollow by the CARRON BURN in BANFFSHIRE. This single Malt Scotch Whisky has a full bodied fruity nose and a smoky finish. For more than a hundred years all distillery supplies were despatched by rail. The steam locomotive "DAILUAINE NO.1" was in use from 1939–1967 and is preserved on the STRATHSPEY RAILWAY.

AGED 16 YEARS

43% vol United & Bottled in SCOTLAND. THE DAILUAINE-TALISKER Co. LTD., DISTILLERS, Scotland, England. 70 cl

- **AGE** -

16 years

- **STRENGTH** -

43%

- **TASTE RATING** -

4

- **COMMENTS** -

This is a rare malt, with a heathery and sweetish flavour.

- **VISITORS** -

The distillery is not open to visitors.

Dailuaine Distillery stands near the Spey below Ben Rinnes and was established in 1851 by William Mackenzie; it was subsequently taken over by his son, Thomas, and greatly expanded during the 1880s. The distillery was one of several owned by the Dailuaine–Talisker Distillery Co., an amalgamated company formed by Mackenzie. Its current owners are United Distillers and most of its produce goes into their blends, such as Johnnie Walker. Consequently, its single malt is still relatively rare, and has only become available in official bottlings in the Distillery (Flora and Fauna) Malts series early in the 1990s.

THE DALMORE

Dalmore Distillery, Alness, Ross-shire

• AGE •

12, 20/26 years

• STRENGTH •

40%

• TASTE RATING •

4

• COMMENTS •

A smooth, full-bodied whisky with a hint of sherry and peat in its malted flavours. A good digestif.

• VISITORS •

Visitors are welcome by appointment at 1100 or 1400 Mon., Tue., Thur., early Sept.– mid June. Telephone 01349-882362 to arrange.

Built in 1839, Dalmore Distillery was bought in 1867 by the Mackenzie family, although ownership has now passed to Whyte & Mackay. Much of its produce today goes into Whyte & Mackay blends. The distillery is attractively set in a picturesque location with a wooded, hilly backdrop and outlook over the Cromarty Firth to the fertile Black Isle. This location led to a break in the production of whisky during the First World War when the American navy took over the distillery and its access to the deepwater Cromarty Firth for the manufacture of mines.

DALWHINNIE

**Dalwhinnie Distillery,
Dalwhinnie, Inverness-shire**

15 years

43%

2–3

*Ideal as a pre- or post-dinner
dram, Dalwhinnie is light and
aromatic with a soft, heather-
honey finish.*

*Visitors are welcome
0930–1700 Mon.–Fri.
Telephone 01528-522264.*

B uilt in 1898 at the end of the
boom years for the whisky
industry, what is today Dalwhinnie
Distillery was called Strathspey when
it first opened, even though it was
not, strictly speaking, on Speyside.
It stands on the Drumochter Pass at
a height of more than 1000 feet,
close to pure water sources, and was
for many years Scotland's highest
distillery. It is presently owned by
United Distillers. Most of its output
went to blending until 1988 when
the Dalwhinnie single malt was
developed.

DEANSTON

**Deanston Distillery,
Doune, Perthshire**

● **AGE** ●

12, 17, 25 years

● **STRENGTH** ●

40%

● **TASTE RATING** ●

3

● **COMMENTS** ●

A light, fresh, smooth Highland malt with a sweetish, fruity flavour.

● **VISITORS** ●

The distillery is not open to visitors.

Originally a cotton mill dating from 1785, Deanston was converted to a whisky distillery in 1966. Water for distilling and electricity comes from the River Teith that rises north of Loch Lomond and flows through the Trossachs. The mill's original weaving sheds, with their humidity control and their temperature, are perfect for maturing the whisky and are considered to add a natural smoothness to its character. Deanston was bought by Burn Stewart of Glasgow in 1991.

DEWAR'S WHITE LABEL

United Distillers, Banbeath, Leven, Fife

● STRENGTH ●

40%

● TASTE RATING ●

2

● COMMENTS ●

Dewar's White Label, the best-selling Scotch whisky in the USA, has a slightly smoky aroma and a complex, delicate, malty flavour with a clean, dry finish.

John Dewar & Sons was one of the blending companies instrumental in the development of new whisky markets outside Scotland. Begun in Perth in 1846, it was the first company to sell its whisky in bottles as well as casks, thus opening up a new market in the home rather than just licensed premises. Dewars was also a pioneer of whisky advertising and was one of the first companies whose bottles carried its company name. More than 90% of production is exported.

BLEND

DIMPLE

**United Distillers,
Banbeath, Leven, Fife**

• AGE •

15 years

• STRENGTH •

40%

• TASTE RATING •

2-3

• COMMENTS •

In its distinctive triangular bottle, Dimple is a good-quality de luxe blend which is also a leader in its market in the UK. More sophisticated than the standard Haig blend, it has a mellow sweetness which is harmoniously balanced by a smoky, peaty flavour.

Haig is a family name long associated with the whisky industry, going back almost 350 years, when Robert Haig, a farmer of Stirlingshire, was rebuked by his local kirk session for distilling his whisky on a Sunday. The Haigs were instrumental in introducing new practices and machinery (for example the new patent still) to the grain distilleries which they built in Edinburgh and elsewhere in the east. Haig was acquired by United Distillers in 1986 and today holds the licence for Glenkinchie, Glenlossie and Mannochmore malt distilleries, and Cameronbridge grain distillery in Fife.

DRAMBUIE

**Drambuie,
Kirkliston, West Lothian**

• STRENGTH •

40%

• TASTE RATING •

2

• COMMENTS •

*Based on a blend of aged
Scotch whisky (many of
which are 15-17 year old
malts), pure heather honey
and other ingredients from an
ancient family recipe,
Drambuie is a sweet after-
dinner whisky liqueur with a
rich and creamy flavour
complemented by fragrant,
fruity notes.*

• VISITORS •

*The plant is not open to
visitors.*

Drambuie moved from its original home on Skye at the start of this century after the decision was taken to produce the liqueur commercially. Its name from the Gaelic *An Dram buiadch*, meaning 'the drink that satisfies', and is chronicled as being the personal liqueur of Prince Charles Edward Stuart, 'Bonnie Prince Charlie'. After his army's defeat by the Hanoverian army at Culloden in 1746, the prince fled to Skye with a few supporters. Among them was Captain John Mackinnon, a native of Skye, whom the prince is said to have rewarded for his loyalty by giving him his only remaining possession – the recipe for his personal liqueur.

HIGHLAND
SINGLE MALT SCOTCH WHISKY

DUFFTOWN

distillery was established near *Dufftown* at the end of the C19th. The
bright flash of the KINGFISHER can often be seen over the *DULLAN
RIVER*, which flows past the old stone buildings of the distillery on
its way north to the *SPEY*. This single HIGHLAND MALT WHISKY
is typically *SPEYSIDE* in character with a delicate, fragrant,
almost flowery aroma and taste which lingers on the palate.

43% vol   70cl

AGED 15 YEARS

DUFFTOWN

**Dufftown Distillery,
Dufftown, Keith, Banffshire**

• AGE •

15 years

• STRENGTH •

43%

• TASTE RATING •

2-3

• COMMENTS •

*A pleasant Speyside malt with
a delicate, fragrant aroma
which is almost flowery, and a
smooth, sweet taste. Doubles
as a before- or after-dinner
dram.*

• VISITORS •

*Visitors are welcome by
appointment, 0900–1600.
Larger parties should telephone
in advance. Telephone 01340-
820224 to arrange.*

Prettily situated at the water's
edge in the Dullan Glen, this is
one of seven distilleries in and
around Dufftown, a major whisky
production centre with plentiful
resources of water, peat and, previously, barley. Despite the abundance
of fresh water in the glen, there were
disputes in the early years over water
rights, some of which led to the noc-
turnal diversion and re-diversion of
local supplies. The distillery finally
gained the right to draw its supplies
from Jock's Well, a reliable source of
fine, sweet water some distance
away.

DUNHILL
OLD MASTER

**Justerini & Brooks,
London**

• STRENGTH •

43%

• TASTE RATING •

3

• COMMENTS •

*A combination of over thirty
individual whiskies, some
more than twenty years old,
Dunhill Old Master is an
exceptionally smooth, richly
flavoured blend.*

Justerini & Brooks was established
in London by the Italian wine
merchant, Giacomo Justerini, in
1749 and began selling Scotch
whisky thirty years later. In 1962 the
company built on previous
amalgamations by combining with
W. & A. Gilbey to form International
Distillers and Vintners Ltd (IDV).
Grand Metropolitan bought IDV,
then part of Watney Mann &
Truman, in 1972. J&B have created a
range of high-quality premium
whiskies for Alfred Dunhill Ltd,
including Dunhill Centenary,
Dunhill's Celebration Edition and
Dunhill's Gentlemen's Speyside
Blend.

BLEND

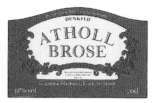

DUNKELD ATHOLL BROSE

Gordon and MacPhail, Elgin, Moray

• AGE •

12 years

• STRENGTH •

35%

• TASTE RATING •

2

• COMMENTS •

Based on a traditional recipe, this liqueur has a good whisky association coming through its sweetness. It is herbal on the nose, with a long, warming finish.

• VISITORS •

Gordon and MacPhail's shop, South St, Elgin is open 0900–1715 Mon.–Wed. (0900–1300 Wed. in winter), 0830–1715 Thu.–Fri., 0900–1700 Sat.

Gordon and MacPhail started in business in 1895 as a licensed grocers and wine and spirit merchant. Unlike many other similar contemporary companies, they have retained all the original aspects of their business as well as extending into vatting, blending and bottling, and are unique in maturing all their whiskies from new. They recently moved into distillation with the purchase of Benromach Distillery from United Distillers. They also produce this liqueur, which won a Silver Award (1985) at the International Wine and Spirit Competition and a Gold Award (1987), when it was named 'the best liqueur in the world'.

THE EDRADOUR

**Edradour Distillery,
Pitlochry, Perthshire**

• AGE •

10 years

• STRENGTH •

40%

• TASTE RATING •

3

• COMMENTS •

*The Edradour is a smooth
Highland malt with pleasant
notes of fruit and malt in its
taste, complemented by a
slight dryness.*

• VISITORS •

*Visitors are welcome.
Telephone 01796-472095 to
arrange.*

B uilt in 1837, Edradour is
Scotland's smallest distillery, as
well as being one of its most
picturesque, standing on the steep
banks of a burn in the Perthshire
countryside. In 1982 it was taken
over by Campbell Distillers, the UK
subsidiary of Pernod Ricard and a
sympathetic modernization that year
kept its traditional appearance. Most
of the malt goes into blends and it is
only since 1986 that The Edradour
has been available as a single malt
under the distillery label.

SINGLE MALT

FAIRLIE'S

**Glenturret Distillery,
The Hosh, Perthshire**

• STRENGTH •

24%

• TASTE RATING •

2

• COMMENTS •

*Smooth and delicate without
being cloying, the secret recipe
used to produce this unique
drink allows the top-grade malt
used to come through.
Excellent as a mixer.*

• VISITORS •

*Visitors are welcome all year.
Telephone 01764-656565.*

Fairlie's Light Highland Liqueur is
produced at Glenturret Distillery,
situated in one of Perthshire's most
spectacular Highland settings. It is
named after the family which did so
much to resurrect the distillery's
fortunes in the 1960s. The label
sports a pouncing cat motif and paw
prints in honour of Towser, the late
distillery cat whose record of 28,899
mice caught in a career lasting
almost twenty-four years earned her
a place in the *Guinness Book of
Records* as the world's most
successful mouser.

THE FAMOUS GROUSE

Matthew Gloag and Son, Perth, Perthshire

• STRENGTH •

40%

• TASTE RATING •

2

• COMMENTS •

The Famous Grouse is a light-to-medium-bodied whisky with a fresh smoothness and a pleasant, lightly peated flavour. It has been the most popular blend in Scotland for several years.

Matthew Gloag & Son began in Perth in 1800 as a licensed grocers, acquiring interests in blending and bottling as the firm expanded during the nineteenth century. What became their most famous product appeared at the end of the century, with the grouse on the name and label successfully capitalizing on the popularity of sporting pastimes among Victorian and Edwardian gentlemen. The blend celebrated its first century in 1995. The company was bought by Highland Distilleries in 1970.

FRASER MCDONALD

Gibson Scotch Whisky Ltd, Glasgow

* STRENGTH *

40%

* TASTE RATING *

2-3

* COMMENTS *

Fraser McDonald is a smooth and mellow blend whose light, fresh taste is underlain by gentle peaty notes.

Fraser McDonald is produced by Gibson Scotch Whisky Co. Ltd, who operate as a subsidiary of the Loch Lomond Distillery Co. Ltd, producers of Inchmurrin single malt. As well as a new grain complex at Loch Lomond, the company holds three malt distilleries: the two Lowland distilleries of Loch Lomond at Alexandria and Littlemill at Bowling, and Glen Scotia in Campbeltown. The latter two have now been mothballed.

GLAYVA

**Glayva Liqueur,
Leith, Edinburgh**

*Glayva, whose name derives
from the Gaelic for 'very
good', is a rich, subtle and
complex liqueur with a hint
of tangerine in its sweet
flavours.*

*The distillery is not open to
visitors.*

Glayva was originally created by
Ronald Morrison & Co., an
Edinburgh merchants well-versed in
flavours and bouquets. The liqueur's
distinctive combination of aged
whisky, syrup of herbs, aromatic oils
and honey took many years to
perfect. The ownership of Glayva
passed to Whyte & Mackay in 1993
when they acquired Invergordon
Distillers, who themselves had
owned the brand since 1984. This
is one of the biggest sellers in the
Scotch whisky liqueur market.

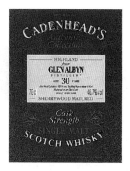

GLEN ALBYN

**Glen Albyn Distillery,
Inverness, Inverness-shire**

• **AGE** •

varies

• **STRENGTH** •

varies

• **TASTE RATING** •

3

• **COMMENTS** •

*This whisky is available from
independent bottlers only and
is difficult to come by. It is a
medium-bodied, smooth malt
with a hint of smokiness in its
bouquet and taste.*

Glen Albyn was first established in 1840, only to be turned into a flour mill after two decades of distilling. It was re-established in the 1880s when a new Glen Albyn Distillery was built on another site close to the Caledonian Canal. The distillery was bought by Mackinlay and Birnie in 1920 and was transferred to Scottish Malt Distillers (SMD), a subsidiary of the Distillers Company Ltd, in 1972. One of several SMD distilleries closed down in 1983, it was subsequently demolished by United Distillers in 1988.

GLENBURGIE

The Glenburgie-Glenlivet Distillery, Forres, Moray

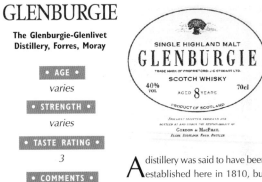

SINGLE HIGHLAND MALT
GLENBURGIE
TRADE MARK OF PROPRIETORS J G STODART LTD

SCOTCH WHISKY

40% VOL — AGED 8 YEARS — 70cl

PRODUCT OF SCOTLAND

SPECIALLY SELECTED, PRODUCED AND BOTTLED BY AND UNDER THE RESPONSIBILITY OF
CORDON & MACPHAIL
ELGIN SCOTLAND REGD BOTTLER

AGE
varies

STRENGTH
varies

TASTE RATING
3

COMMENTS

A light-bodied, delicate single malt whose sweet, slightly floral taste makes it ideal as an aperitif. It is found relatively rarely in this country, as most goes for export.

VISITORS

The distillery has no reception centre but visitors are welcome by appointment. Telephone 01343-850258 to arrange.

A distillery was said to have been established here in 1810, but production ceased and was not revived until the second half of the nineteenth century. It was bought by James & George Stodart Ltd of Dumbarton who themselves were taken over by Hiram Walker in the 1930s. The distillery was extended in 1958 and is now owned by Allied Distillers, with most of its produce going into their blends.

GLENCADAM

**Glencadam Distillery,
Brechin, Angus**

• AGE •

varies

• STRENGTH •

varies

• TASTE RATING •

3-4

• COMMENTS •

Glencadam, generally available from independent whisky merchants, has a delicate, fruity bouquet and rich, sweetish flavour with a smooth, well-rounded finish.

• VISITORS •

The distillery has no reception centre but visitors are welcome by appointment. Telephone 01356-622217 to arrange.

Glencadam, built around 1825, dates from the time of the first wave of licensed distilleries, and was one of two distilleries in Brechin dating from this decade (North Port being the other). It takes its water from Moorfoot Loch. It is owned by Allied Distillers but has only rarely been officially bottled as a single malt, with most of its production going into the Stewarts Cream of the Barley blend .

GLEN CALDER

Gordon and MacPhail, Elgin, Moray

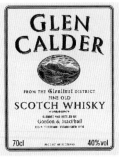

• STRENGTH •

40%

• TASTE RATING •

2

• COMMENTS •

A very pleasant blend with a smooth, honey-like nose and light, slightly smoky finish.

• VISITORS •

Gordon and MacPhail's shop, South St, Elgin is open 0900–1715 Mon.–Wed. (0900–1300 Wed. in winter), 0830–1715 Thu.–Fri., 0900–1700 Sat. Telephone 01340-871471.

Gordon and MacPhail started in business in 1895 as a licensed grocers and wine and spirit merchant, as had done so many of the foremost names among the Scotch whisky blending industry. Unlike the others, however, they have retained all the original aspects of their business as well as extending into vatting, blending and bottling. Glen Calder is one of the most popular blends in northern Scotland and won a Silver Award at the 1981 International Wine and Spirits Competition.

GLEN DEVERON

**Macduff Distillery,
Banff, Banffshire**

* AGE *

5, 10, 12 years

* STRENGTH *

40%

* TASTE RATING *

3-4

* COMMENTS *

Amodern distillery, built in 1960, Macduff is one of the few distilleries to give its single malt a different name from its own. The malt takes its names from the nearby River Deveron from which is drawn the water used for cooling in the production process. Macduff Distillery is now owned by William Lawson Distillers, a subsidiary of Bacardi Ltd, Bermuda.

A very pleasant Highland malt with a smooth, mellow taste and fresh bouquet.

* VISITORS *

Visitors are welcome by appointment. Telephone 01261-812612 to arrange.

GLENDRONACH

**The Glendronach Distillery,
Forgue, Huntly, Aberdeenshire**

• AGE •

15 years

• STRENGTH •

40%, 43%

• TASTE RATING •

3

• COMMENTS •

*Glendronach is a beautifully
rounded single malt whose
slight peaty tones are balanced by a lingering
sweetness.*

• VISITORS •

*Visitors are welcome by
appointment. Telephone
01466-730202 to arrange.*

This distillery, set picturesquely
on the Dronach Burn in the
Aberdeenshire countryside, is one of
the most attractive in the Highlands.
Built in 1826, it was one of the first to
be licensed, and its whisky enjoyed
a wide reputation in the nineteenth
century. Its original hand-turned
malting floor and coal-fired stills
have been retained. Since 1960 it
has been operated by William
Teacher & Sons, with produce going
into the Teacher's blends. It has been
owned since 1988 by Allied
Distillers who have temporarily
suspended production.

SPEYSIDE
SINGLE MALT
SCOTCH WHISKY

GLENDULLAN

distillery, located in a beautiful wooded
valley near ... built in 1897 and is one of seven
established in Dufftown in the 19th.
The River Fiddich flows past the distillery,
originally providing power to drive
machinery, it is now used ... for cooling.
GLENDULLAN is a firm, mellow single MALT
SCOTCH WHISKY with a fruity
bouquet and a smooth lingering finish.

AGED 12 YEARS

43% vol   70cl

GLENDULLAN

**Glendullan Distillery,
Dufftown, Keith, Banffshire**

◆ AGE ◆

12 years

◆ STRENGTH ◆

43%

◆ TASTE RATING ◆

3

◆ COMMENTS ◆

*A good single malt with a
robust character yet a mellow,
fruity flavour.*

◆ VISITORS ◆

*Visitors are welcome by
appointment. Telephone
01340-820250 to arrange.*

This is one of the seven Dufftown
distilleries, built just before the
turn of the century and picturesquely
set on the banks of the Fiddich. Built
for William Williams of Aberdeen, it
passed to the control of Macdonald
Greenlees & Williams after the First
World War and, with its parent
company, into the ownership of the
Distillers Company Ltd in 1926. It is
now owned by United Distillers and
its single malt is still relatively rare,
although it has been officially bottled
in the Distillery (Flora and Fauna)
Malts series. Glendullan is also an
important component of Old Parr and
of President, a de luxe blend.

SINGLE MALT

GLENFARCLAS

**Glenfarclas Distillery,
Marypark, Ballindalloch,
Banffshire**

• AGE •

10, 12, 15, 21, 25, 30 years

• STRENGTH •

40%, 43%, 46%, 60%

• TASTE RATING •

3–4, 5 (60%)

• COMMENTS •

*This is widely acknowledged
as one of the classic malts. It
has a rich, sherry bouquet, a
well-rounded, fruity body and
a delicious, mellow finish.*

• VISITORS •

*Visitors are welcome
0900–1630 Mon.–Fri.,
1000–1600 Sat., June–Sept.,
1000–1600 Mon.–Fri., Oct.–
May; or by appointment. Large
parties should telephone in
advance. Telephone 01807-
500209.*

Glenfarclas is one of the few
independently owned distilleries left in the Highlands. Founded
in 1836, it was bought in 1865 by J.
& G. Grant (who were no direct
relations of the family of Grants at
Glenfiddich) and is still in family
hands. Glenfarclas bottles a wide
range of malts of varying ages and
strengths. The distillery is set in an
isolated spot by Ben Rinnes yet it
attracts in excess of 60,000 visitors a
year to its well-maintained visitor
facilities.

SINGLE MALT

GLENFIDDICH

**Glenfiddich Distillery,
Dufftown, Keith, Banffshire**

• AGE •

No age given

• STRENGTH •

40%

• TASTE RATING •

2

• COMMENTS •

Glenfiddich has a light, peaty aroma with a smooth, counter-balancing sweetness. It offers an excellent introduction to malt whisky, and is ideal, too, as an aperitif.

• VISITORS •

Visitors are welcome 0930–1630 Mon.–Fri. all year; 0930–1630 Sat., 1200–1630 Sun., Easter–mid Oct. Large parties should telephone in advance. Telephone 01340-820373.

Glenfiddich Distillery was started by William Grant, a former apprentice shoemaker who worked at Mortlach, another Dufftown distillery, until he gained enough knowledge and money to set up on his own in 1887. The new distillery was successful as soon as it went into production, and has remained so ever since, thanks not only to the quality and accessibility of its product but also to far-sighted marketing which has made its single malt one of the best-known in the world.

GLEN GARIOCH

Glen Garioch Distillery, Oldmeldrum, Aberdeenshire

• AGE •
8, 15, 21 years

• STRENGTH •
40%, 43%

• TASTE RATING •
3

• COMMENTS •

This medium-bodied whisky, with its light texture and smoky flavour, is an ideal after-dinner dram.

Set in the small Aberdeenshire market town of Oldmeldrum, Glen Garioch was reputedly founded in the 1790s. It has had several owners throughout its history, and was sold by the Distillers Company Ltd in 1970 to Morrison Bowmore, two years after its closure because of a shortage of water. Having sunk a new well, Morrison were able to tap sufficient sources of spring water to enable normal production to continue. Mothballed in 1995, production was restarted in 1997.

SINGLE MALT

GLENGOYNE

**Glengoyne Distillery,
Dumgoyne, Stirlingshire**

• AGE •

10, 17, 21 years

• STRENGTH •

40%, 43%

• TASTE RATING •

2-3

• COMMENTS •

A light, pleasant, sweetish whisky with a fragrant aroma and no abrasive edges. Ideal as an aperitif.

• VISITORS •

Visitors are welcome during working hours, Mon.–Sun. Large parties (of ten and over) are requested to book ahead. Telephone 01360-550254 to arrange.

Glengoyne stands just north of the Highland Line (the line initiated by the Customs and Excise to differentiate area boundaries between styles of whisky) and so qualifies as a Highland distillery. It was built in 1833 at the foot of the Campsie Fells, near the fifty-foot waterfall from which it takes its supplies. It was bought by Lang Brothers in 1876 and was sympathetically restored and extended in the 1960s.

GLEN GRANT

Glen Grant Distillery, Rothes, Moray

• AGE •

No age, 5, 10 years

• STRENGTH •

40%, 43%

• TASTE RATING •

2

• COMMENTS •

The 5-year-old is light and dry, making it ideal as an aperitif, while the older version has a sweeter, fruitier, more rounded character.

• VISITORS •

Visitors are welcome 1000–1600 Mon.–Sat., and from 1130 Sun., mid Mar.–Oct.;1000-1700,Mon-Sat., and 1130-1700, Sun., June to end Sepetmber. Telephone 01542-783318.

Opened by James and John Grant in 1840, Glen Grant enjoyed continuous expansion throughout the last century, and this has continued to the present day. The company was amalgamated with the Smiths of Glenlivet in the 1950s to form The Glenlivet and Glen Grant Distillers, which in turn merged with the Edinburgh blending firm of Hill Thomson in 1970 to form The Glenlivet Distillers. Glen Grant is now part of Seagram. The distillery's Five Years Old single malt is the best-selling malt whisky in Italy.

PRODUCE OF SCOTLAND

GLENKEITH

SINGLE HIGHLAND MALT
Scotch Whisky

Distilled before

1983

A fragrant whisky
from the heart of
the Highlands,
GLEN KEITH
is prized by
experts for its
purity and depth
of flavour.

GLEN KEITH
is matured for
more than ten
years in oak casks.
The whisky is then
further under the
supervision of our
Head Distiller.

The peal of the Salmon

The Glen Keith distillery stands beside the fast-flowing river Isla,
above a deep pool where wild salmon swim and leap. The Gaelic name is
"linn a' bhradain." Here, nature is unspoilt, the air and the water pure and
sweet. It is in the very heart of Scotch Whisky country.

70 cl ℮   BOTTLED IN SCOTLAND   43%vol

GLEN KEITH

**Glen Keith Distillery,
Keith, Banffshire**

- • AGE •
varies

- • STRENGTH •
43%

- • TASTE RATING •
2

- • COMMENTS •
*A difficult-to-find, smooth and
sweet-tasting Speyside single
malt which is occasionally
available from independent
bottlers.*

- • VISITORS •
*The distillery is open by
appointment. Telephone
01542-783042 to arrange.*

Glen Keith was built by Chivas
Brothers in 1958, across the
River Isla from Strathisla, another of
their distilleries and one of the oldest
in Scotland. As if by deliberate
contrast, processes used at Glen
Keith are innovative, and it was the
first of the Scotch whisky distilleries
to have its production processes
automated. Unlike the usual
practice, distillations are not bottled
at fixed ages but are individually
selected at what is judged to be the
optimum point in the maturation
process.

SINGLE MALT

GLENKINCHIE

**Glenkinchie Distillery,
Pencaitland, Tranet,
East Lothian**

* AGE *

10 years

* STRENGTH *

43%

* TASTE RATING *

3

* COMMENTS *

*Ideal as an aperitif,
Glenkinchie, the Edinburgh
malt, is the driest and smokiest
of Lowland whiskies. It is a
fine, pale, smooth whisky.*

* VISITORS *

*Visitors are welcome
0930–1630 Mon.–Fri.
Telephone 01875-340333.*

Glenkinchie takes its name from the burn which flows by it and the glen in which it stands. It was established in the late 1830s and has been in production since, except during the wars. The licence is held by Haig, the brand owned by United Distillers, and most of Glenkinchie's product goes into their blends. The single malt was officially bottled by United Distillers in their Classic Malts series.

THE GLENLIVET

The Glenlivet Distillery, Ballindalloch, Banffshire

• AGE •

12, 18, 21 years

• STRENGTH •

40%, 43%

• TASTE RATING •

3–4

• COMMENTS •

The Glenlivet is a subtly balanced malt. Its light, delicate bouquet has traces of fruit, and floral notes, while the complex flavours are delicately balanced between a medium sweetness and smooth dryness.

• VISITORS •

Visitors are welcome 1000– 1600 Mon.–Sat, Sun. 1230- 1600, mid Mar.–end Oct., until 1800 daily, July–Aug. Telephone 01542-783220.

This was one of the first distilleries licensed under the reforming 1823 Licensing Act – a fact which so incensed his still-illegal neighbours that its founder, George Smith, was obliged to carry pistols for his own protection. The whisky so grew in popularity that other distillers adopted the name, and an ensuing legal case and settlement (which endures to this day) allowed the Smiths to use the direct article in their whisky's name while others were to use it as a hyphenated suffix.

GLENLOCHY

Glenochy Distillery, Fort William, Inverness-shire

- **AGE**
  varies
- **STRENGTH**
  varies
- **TASTE RATING**
  2
- **COMMENTS**

A floral bouquet leads into a clean, dryish-tasting malt with a rather quick finish. Light-bodied and good as an aperitif.

CONNOISSEURS CHOICE

Connoisseurs Choice, a range of single malts from various districts of Scotland

In the Highlands are situated the greatest number of malt whisky distilleries

SINGLE HIGHLAND MALT SCOTCH WHISKY
DISTILLED AT
GLENLOCHY
DISTILLERY
PROPRIETORS: D. & J. McCallum Ltd

DISTILLED **1977** DISTILLED

SPECIALLY SELECTED, PRODUCED AND BOTTLED BY
70cl   GORDON & MACPHAIL   40%vol.
ELGIN SCOTLAND
PRODUCT OF SCOTLAND

Glenlochy Distillery was built close to Loch Lochy at the southern end of the Caledonian Canal in a pretty setting on the outskirts of Fort William. It was built in 1900 with production beginning the following year. The single malt is now something of a rarity, as almost all of the distillery's produce went into blends. The situation will not improve, as Glenlochy was closed by its parent company, United Distillers, in the 1980s, and sold outside the industry in 1991.

GLENLOSSIE

Glenlossie-Glenlivet Distillery, Birnie, Elgin, Moray

• AGE •

10 years

• STRENGTH •

43%

• TASTE RATING •

2

• COMMENTS •

Another whisky which is difficult to find, Glenlossie has a fresh, grassy aroma with a touch of fruitiness and a smooth, lingering flavour.

• VISITORS •

Visitors are welcome by appointment. Telephone 01343-86331 to arrange.

Glenlossie was built not far from the River Lossie in 1876 by a former distillery manager-turned-hotel owner from Lhanbryde, near Elgin. It was expanded and improved between 1896 and 1917. In 1962, its stills were increased from four to six, while in 1992 a new mash tun was fitted. The licensee is presently Haig and the distillery is owned by United Distillers. The single malt is still relatively rare, but became available in official bottlings in UD's Distillery (Flora and Fauna) Malts series early in the 1990s.

GLEN MHOR

**Glen Mhor Distillery,
Inverness, Inverness-shire**

• AGE •
varies

• STRENGTH •
varies

• TASTE RATING •
3

• COMMENTS •

*Smooth and medium-bodied,
Glen Mhor has a pleasant,
subtle sweetness comple-
mented by a dryish, heathery
aftertaste.*

This distillery was built between
1892 and 1894 by Mackinlay
and Birnie who were later to own
the neighbouring Glen Albyn
Distillery; John Birnie had previously managed Glen Albyn. Glen Mhor
used the same water (from Loch
Ness) and peat as its neighbour, but
their whiskies were quite different.
It was one of the first distilleries in
Scotland to introduce mechanical
malting in the late 1940s. It was
closed down by the Distillers
Company Ltd in 1983 and
demolished in 1988.

GLENMORANGIE

Glenmorangie Distillery, Tain, Ross-shire

• AGE •
10, 18 years

• STRENGTH •
40%, 43%

• TASTE RATING •
3-4

• COMMENTS •
A smooth and medium-bodied whisky, with a delicate, slightly sweet aroma. Scotland's best-selling single malt.

• VISITORS •
Visitors are welcome 1000–1600 Mon.–Fri. all year and 1000–1600 Sat. Jun.–Oct. Booking is advisable. Telephone 01862-892477 to arrange.

Distilling was begun here in 1843 by the Mathieson family as a sideline to farming. In 1918, The Glenmorangie Distillery Company passed into the control of its present owners, Macdonald and Muir Ltd. Water is supplied by unusually hard, mineral-rich springs in nearby Tarlogie Forest, and the lightly peated new spirit is distilled in Glenmorangie's characteristically tall, swan-necked stills, before being transferred into charred American oak barrels for the maturation process.

SINGLE MALT

GLENMORANGIE PORT WOOD FINISH

Glenmorangie Distillery, Tain, Ross-shire

• AGE •

at least 12 years

• STRENGTH •

43%

• TASTE RATING •

3

• COMMENTS •

This whisky has a sweet aroma with minty notes and a dry, very smooth taste. The port flavours of the final maturing process come through on the lingering and quite satisfying finish.

• VISITORS •

Visitors are welcome 1000–1600 Mon.–Fri., Apr.–Oct., 1400–1600 Mon-Fri., Nov.–Mar., or by appointment. Telephone 01862-892477 to arrange.

This malt is one of a series of newcomers to Glenmorangie's single malts range. In its final 'finishing' period of maturation, the whisky is transferred not into the usual charred American oak bourbon barrels, but into casks which have previously contained port. This second wood imparts its own new qualities which enhance, without overpowering, the delicate and subtle core flavours. Glenmorangie also produce two other single malts which have been finished in madeira and sherry casks.

GLEN MORAY

Glen Moray Distillery, Elgin, Moray

• AGE •
12, 16 years

• STRENGTH •
40%, 43%

• TASTE RATING •
2-3

• COMMENTS •
Golden in colour, with a soft, fresh bouquet leading into a smooth and rounded taste, Glen Moray is a classic Speyside malt.

Established during the whisky boom years of the 1890s, the Glen Moray Distillery was expanded in 1958. Since the 1920s it has been owned by Macdonald & Muir Ltd and, in addition to its availability as a single malt, its produce also features in many well-known blends. Glen Moray is the sister distillery to the better-known Glenmorangie.

• VISITORS •
Visitors are welcome by appointment. Telephone 01343-542577 to arrange.

GLEN ORD

**Glen Ord Distillery,
Muir of Ord, Ross-shire**

• AGE •
12 years

• STRENGTH •
40%

• TASTE RATING •
2–3

• COMMENTS •

A smooth, well-rounded and slightly dry malt with a fragrant bouquet and mellow finish.

• VISITORS •

Visitors are welcome 0930–1700 Mon.–Fri. Telephone 01463-870421.

This distillery stands in an area which was infamous for illicit distillation even as late as a century ago. It stands on a tributary of the River Conan, the Oran Burn, whose clear waters have been used by legal and illegal whisky producers alike. Ord Distillery, as it then was, was founded in 1838 on land leased from the Mackenzies of Ord to provide a ready market for barley produced on Mackenzie farms. It was acquired by Dewar in 1923, and is now owned by United Distillers.

SINGLE MALT

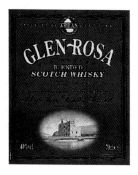

GLEN ROSA

Isle of Arran Distillers, Mauchline, Ayrshire

• STRENGTH •

40%

• TASTE RATING •

2-3

• COMMENTS •

A medium-dry whisky with soft aromas of sweet, oaky vanilla and a dark peatiness. It is full-bodied, but gentle and smooth with a smoky note to its finish.

Isle of Arran Distillers are a dynamic new player in the Scotch whisky industry. Independent and family-run, the company has a portfolio of blended and malt whiskies which has been successfully marketed throughout Europe, the Americas and Asia. In 1995 the company opened a new distillery on Arran at Lochranza and its first produce is presently maturing, with an expected launch as a single malt early in the new millennium.

THE GLENROTHES

Glen Rothes Distillery, Rothes, Moray

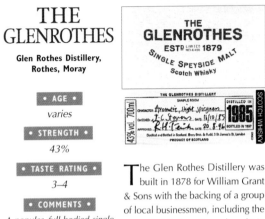

THE
GLENROTHES
ESTD LIMITED 1879
RELEASE
SINGLE SPEYSIDE MALT
Scotch Whisky

THE GLENROTHES DISTILLERY
SAMPLE ROOM
CHARACTER *Aromatic, slight Spicyness*
CHECKED *I.C. Stevens* DATE *11/10/85*
APPROVED *R.H. Tenith* DATE *20. 8. 96*
Distilled and Bottled in Scotland. Berry Bros. & Rudd, 3 St. James's St, London
PRODUCT OF SCOTLAND

43% vol. 700ml

DISTILLED IN
1985
BOTTLED IN 1997

SCOTCH WHISKY

---

* **AGE** *

varies

* **STRENGTH** *

43%

* **TASTE RATING** *

3–4

* **COMMENTS** *

A popular, full-bodied single malt with a delicate, lightly peated aroma and a pleasingly smooth aftertaste.

* **VISITORS** *

The distillery is not open to visitors.

The Glen Rothes Distillery was built in 1878 for William Grant & Sons with the backing of a group of local businessmen, including the provost of Rothes. It was bought in 1887 by the Islay Distillery Company, owners of Bunnahabhain, and then became part of the Highland Distilleries company. They still own the distillery today. Glen Rothes has been expanded twice in the last thirty years. The Glen Rothes vintage single malt is produced and distributed by Berry Brothers & Rudd, the owners of Cutty Sark whisky, in which Glen Rothes also features.

SINGLE MALT

GLEN SCOTIA

Glen Scotia Distillery, Campbeltown, Argyll

• **AGE** •
12 years

• **STRENGTH** •
40%

• **TASTE RATING** •
3

• **COMMENTS** •
Glen Scotia is a rich, peaty, oily malt with a pungent aroma and a smooth, well-rounded finish.

• **VISITORS** •
The distillery is not open to visitors.

Scotia, as it was previously known, was one of thirty-two Campbeltown distilleries operating last century, partly explaining why the town has its own regional classification, even though only two distilleries remain. Glen Scotia Distillery was built in 1835 and has had many owners, the ghost of one of whom is said to haunt the place. It is currently owned by Loch Lomond Distillery Co. Ltd, the owners of Loch Lomond Distillery and the producers of Inchmurrin single malt. Both Glen Scotia and its sister distillery, Littlemill at Bowling, have now been mothballed.

GLENTAUCHERS

**Glentauchers Distillery,
Mulben, Banffshire**

- **AGE** •

varies

- **STRENGTH** •

40%

- **TASTE RATING** •

2

- **COMMENTS** •

The sweetness of Glentauchers' aroma and taste are balanced by the light dryness of its finish. A nice pre-dinner dram, but generally available only from independent merchants.

- **VISITORS** •

The distillery has no reception centre but visitors are welcome by appointment. Telephone 01542-860272 to arrange.

Glentauchers was built in 1898 by James Buchanan, the entrepreneur responsible for the success of Black & White whisky, and its product went into their blends. Buchanan's distillery was largely rebuilt and modernized in 1965 but was silent for several years in the 1980s until Allied Distillers acquired it from United Distillers in 1988 and immediately reopened it.

THE GLENTURRET

Glenturret Distillery, The Hosh, Crieff, Perthshire

• AGE •

12, 15, 18, 21, 25 years

• STRENGTH •

40%

• TASTE RATING •

3–4

• COMMENTS •

Glenturret is an award-winning, full-bodied Highland malt with a rich, nutty flavour and nicely rounded finish.

• VISITORS •

Visitors are welcome all year. Telephone 01764-656565.

Glenturret stands in a lovely position on the banks of the River Turret, in an area where smuggling and illicit distillation were rife in the past. It is probable that the distillery's own eighteenth-century origins lie there; some of its buildings date from that time. Glenturret was closed and partially dismantled in the 1920s until 1959, when it was largely rebuilt, anticipating the huge upswing in demand for blended whiskies in the 1960s. Today its visitor facilities are among the best of any Scots whisky distillery.

THE GLENTURRET
ORIGINAL
MALT LIQUEUR

**Glenturret Distillery,
The Hosh, Crieff, Perthshire**

The Glenturret Original Malt
Liqueur is produced at Scotland's
oldest working distillery, officially
established in 1775 but with a history
predating this by some sixty years.
Glenturret Distillery stands in a
lovely position on the banks of the
River Turret, in an area where
smuggling and illicit distillation were
rife in the past. Glenturret was closed
from the 1920s until 1959, when it
was largely rebuilt and its fortunes
restored under the direction of the
Fairlie family. Facilities for visitors
are among the best of any distillery.

GLENUGIE

Glenugie Distillery, Peterhead, Aberdeenshire

CADENHEAD'S

HIGHLAND

from
Glenugie
Distillery

AGED **18** YEARS

Distilled April 1978, and Bottled January 1997
Matured in Oak Cask
DISTILLED IN SCOTLAND

70cl   58.3% vol.

HIGHLAND

Cask Strength

SCOTCH WHISKY

• AGE •
varies

• STRENGTH •
varies

• TASTE RATING •
2

• COMMENTS •

A medium-bodied whisky with a sweetish, malty flavour and a fruity aroma. Although there were never any official bottlings under the its own label, supplies from the independent merchants are still available.

Glenugie was the easternmost distillery in Scotland, located in Peterhead, the fishing capital of the north-east. The distillery was first established in the 1830s, and was completely rebuilt in 1875. Although enjoyable, its produce never attained the status of a classic. Glenugie Distillery was closed permanently in 1982 and sold outside the industry. Although there were never any official bottlings under the its own label, supplies from the independent merchants are still available.

SINGLE MALT

GRAND MACNISH

Macduff International, Glasgow

- • BOTTLING AGE •

12 years, 18 years

- • STRENGTH •

40%, 43%

- • TASTE RATING •

2

- • COMMENTS •

A light, very smooth blend in which the sweetness of the predominantly Highland whiskies comes through on the finish.

- • VISITORS •

The blending and bottling plant is not open to visitors.

Grand MacNish is produced by Macduff International Ltd, an independent Scotch whisky company. The brand was first established by Robert McNish in 1863, the early days of whisky-blending. It is presently available as a standard blend, a twelve-year-old, and an eighteen-year-old.

BLEND

HAIG

**United Distillers,
Banbeath, Leven, Fife**

• STRENGTH •

43%

• TASTE RATING •

2

• COMMENTS •

A nicely balanced whisky with a fragrant aroma, Haig is smooth and easy to drink, with a long, sweet finish.

Haig is a family name long associated with the whisky industry, going back almost 350 years, when Robert Haig, a farmer of Stirlingshire, was rebuked by his local kirk session for distilling his whisky on a Sunday. The family had connections by marriage to the Steins, another of the big Lowland distilling families, and the Jamesons, the Dublin whiskey distillers. The company was acquired by the Distillers Company in 1919 and is now owned by United Distillers.

HEATHER CREAM

**Moffat Distillery,
Airdrie, Lanarkshire**

- STRENGTH -

17%

- TASTE RATING -

2

- COMMENTS -

*Heather Cream is a sweet
blend of cream and malt
whisky, and is one of the most
popular of the Scotch whisky
cream liqueurs available
today.*

- VISITORS -

*The distillery and plant are not
open to visitors.*

Heather Cream's producers, Inver House Distillers, also produce Pinwinnie de luxe blend, among others. They are owners of Knockdhu (producing An Cnoc single malt) and Speyburn-Glenlivet distilleries, and have recently added to their complement of malt distilleries by buying Pultney and Balblair from Allied Distillers. Heather Cream is produced at their complex at Moffat Distillery on the outskirts of Airdrie, a converted former paper mill.

HIGHLAND PARK

Highland Park Distillery, Kirkwall, Orkney

• AGE •
12 years

• STRENGTH •
40%

• TASTE RATING •
3–4

• COMMENTS •
Highland Park is a medium-bodied single malt of character, with a heathery–smoky aroma and peaty flavour with balancing sweet tones.

• VISITORS •
Visitors are welcome 1000–1700 Mon.–Fri., Apr.–Oct., and 1200– 1700 Sat. & Sun., Jul.–Aug. Large groups should book in advance. Telephone 01856-874619 to arrange, and for details of winter opening.

Highland Park's origins are linked with an illegal bothy which previously occupied the site. Its owner was one of whisky's most colourful characters, Magnus Eunson. A United Presbyterian church elder by day and smuggler by night, his piety did not prevent his using the church pulpit as a handy hiding place for his illicit distillations. The distillery was founded in 1798 and passed to the Grant family in 1895. Highland Distilleries purchased it in 1937. The different nature of Orcadian peat is said to be a factor in the quite distinctive qualities of the islands' whiskies.

IMMORTAL MEMORY

**Gordon and MacPhail,
Elgin, Moray**

• AGE •
8 years

• STRENGTH •
40%

• TASTE RATING •
2

• COMMENTS •
A blend which is floral on the nose – perhaps with a hint of parma violets – with a nutty flavour and a warming finish.

• VISITORS •
Gordon and MacPhail's shop, South St, Elgin is open 0900–1715 Mon.–Wed. (0900–1300 Wed. in winter), 0830–1715 Thu.–Fri., 0900–1700 Sat.

Gordon and MacPhail began in 1895 as a licensed grocers and wine and spirit merchant, as had done so many of the foremost names among the Scotch whisky blending industry. Unlike the others, however, Gordon and MacPhail have retained all the original aspects of their business as well as extending into vatting, blending and bottling. This blend was declared 'Best Blended Whisky in the World' at the 1991 International Wine and Spirit Competition.

BLEND

IMPERIAL

**Imperial Distillery,
Carron, Moray**

• AGE •
varies

• STRENGTH •
varies

• TASTE RATING •
4

• COMMENTS •
A full-bodied malt with bags of character, Imperial contrives to balance a rich sweetness with a lingering smokiness. Available from independent merchants.

• VISITORS •
The distillery has no reception centre but visitors are welcome by appointment. Telephone 01340-810276 to arrange.

The patriotically named Imperial Distillery was first established in 1897, the year of Queen Victoria's Diamond Jubilee. Its founder was Thomas Mackenzie, who was already the owner of Dailuaine and Talisker distilleries. All three were brought together under the name of Dailuaine-Talisker Distilleries Ltd. Imperial Distillery was modernized in the mid 1950s. Production was halted temporarily in the 1980s, but was restarted again after Imperial's purchase by Allied Distillers in 1988.

INCHGOWER

**Inchgower Distillery,
Buckie, Banffshire**

• AGE •
14 years

• STRENGTH •
43%

• TASTE RATING •
2–3

• COMMENTS •

A robust, distinctly heavy-bodied malt with a combination of nutty, fruity and spicy aromas, and a hint of sweetness in its tones.

• VISITORS •

Visitors are welcome by appointment. Telephone 01542-831161.

Inchgower Distillery was moved from Tochineal by its founder, Alexander Wilson, to its present site at Rathaven near Buckie, to take advantage of the ready supply of water from the Letter Burn and the Springs of Aultmoor. When the original firm went out of business, the distillery passed to Buckie Town Council who sold it to Arthur Bell & Sons for £1000 in 1938. Most of the whisky goes into Bell's blends and the distillery is now owned by United Distillers.

SINGLE MALT

INCHMURRIN

SINGLE HIGHLAND MALT

SCOTCH WHISKY

Distilled by
THE LOCH LOMOND DISTILLERY
DUNBARTONSHIRE SCOTLAND

70cle   40%vol
PRODUCT OF SCOTLAND

INCHMURRIN

**Loch Lomond Distillery,
Alexandria, Dunbartonshire**

• AGE •
10 years

• STRENGTH •
40%

• TASTE RATING •
2

• COMMENTS •

A clean, light, pre-dinner malt with a fresh, floral note. A Highland malt with a Lowland character.

• VISITORS •

The distillery is not open to visitors.

A relatively recent addition to the ranks of Scotland's distilleries, Loch Lomond Distillery was founded in 1966 on the site of an old printing and bleaching plant. Like Glengoyne, it just qualifies as being a Highland malt and is situated just to the south of the famous loch. A grain distillery now shares the site. Its present owners, Loch Lomond Distillery Co., recently took control of two more malt distilleries, Littlemill at Bowling and Glen Scotia in Campbeltown, both of which are currently mothballed.

INVERGORDON

Invergordon Distillery, Invergordon, Ross-shire

• AGE •

10 years

• STRENGTH •

40%

• TASTE RATING •

1

• COMMENTS •

A light, clean, smooth whisky with a gentle, slightly vanilla-like taste.

• VISITORS •

The distillery is not open to visitors.

Built in the late 1950s to provide work in an area of high unemployment, Invergordon grain distillery is now one of the biggest distilleries in Europe. Like other distilleries in the area, a provost of Inverness had a hand in its establishment. Along with the seven former Invergordon Distillers' malt distilleries, this giant grain complex was acquired in 1993 by Whyte & Mackay. Ben Wyvis malt distillery was added on the same site but is now closed.

GRAIN

INVERLEVEN

**Inverleven Distillery,
Dumbarton, Dunbartonshire**

• AGE •

varies

• STRENGTH •

varies

• TASTE RATING •

2

• COMMENTS •

A relatively smooth Lowland malt, with a nice balance of dry and sweet flavours. Available from independent whisky merchants only.

• VISITORS •

The distillery is not suitable for visitors.

Built in 1938, Inverleven is part of a modern-looking, multi-storey red-brick plant, which includes Dumbarton grain distillery, on the banks of the Leven in Dumbarton. It stands on the Highland Line (the line initiated by the Customs and Excise to differentiate area boundaries between styles of whisky), and is classified as a Lowland distillery. It is owned by Allied Distillers and almost all of its output goes into their blends, which include the popular Ballantine's, Teacher's and Long John blends.

ISLAND PRINCE

**Isle of Arran Distillers Ltd,
Mauchline, Ayrshire**

• STRENGTH •

40%

• TASTE RATING •

2–3

• COMMENTS •

*A very smooth blend of very
old malt and grains, the
youngest of which is 15 years
old, this has a delicate, slightly
sweet aroma with peaty notes
coming through on the finish.*

Isle of Arran Distillers are a dynamic
new player in the Scotch whisky
industry. Independent and family-
run, the company has a portfolio of
blended and malt whiskies which
has been successfully marketed
throughout Europe, the Americas
and Asia. In 1995, the company
opened a new distillery on Arran at
Lochranza and its first produce is
presently maturing, with an expected
launch as a single malt early in the
new millennium.

BLEND

• AGE •

8, 12, 17 years

• STRENGTH •

40%, 43%

• TASTE RATING •

3

• COMMENTS •

The blenders of Islay Mist, Macduff International, are an independent Scotch whisky company. This mellow Islay de luxe blend made its first appearance in 1928 to mark the 21st birthday of Lord Margadale. As well as Islay Mist, their product range includes Lauder's, one of the oldest blends in the Scotch whisky market, as well as Grand MacNish and Strathbeag blends.

This de luxe blend instantly betrays its origins, though as the name suggests, it is mellower in taste than its main component, Laphroaig. Islay Mist is matured in oak casks and is ideal as an introduction for those wishing to sample the delights of the Islay whiskies.

• VISITORS •

The blending and bottling plant is not open to visitors.

ISLE OF JURA

**Isle of Jura Distillery,
Craighouse, Jura, Argyll**

• AGE •

10 years

• STRENGTH •

40%, 43%

• TASTE RATING •

3

• COMMENTS •

Reminiscent of a Highland malt, though with a light, clean, fragrant palate of its own, this unique Island malt is ideal as an aperitif.

• VISITORS •

Visitors are welcome by appointment. Telephone 01496-820240 to arrange.

The distillery was first built overlooking the Sound of Jura in 1810. The distillery's machinery and buildings were owned by different individuals, and a dispute between the two led to its closure for over fifty years in 1913. It was effectively redesigned and rebuilt before its reopening in the 1960s. The present owners are Whyte & Mackay who acquired it, and six other malt distilleries, after their purchase of Invergordon Distillers in 1993.

SINGLE MALT

J&B JET

Justerini & Brooks, London

• STRENGTH •

43%

• TASTE RATING •

3

• COMMENTS •

Jet has fresh, fragrant aroma which leads into a rich, mellow taste with unexpected sweet notes.

Giacomo Justerini, was a wine merchant from Bologna who set up the wine merchants, Justerini and Brooks in the capital in 1749 and began selling Scotch thirty years later. In 1962 the company built on previous amalgamations by combining with W. & A. Gilbey to form International Distillers and Vintners Ltd (IDV). Grand Metropolitan bought IDV in 1972. Jet took J&B twelve years to develop as a major product in the premium Scotch market. A high proportion of Speyside malts is used in its blend of twelve- and fifteen-year-old whiskies.

J&B RARE

Justerini & Brooks, London

• STRENGTH •

40%, 43%

• TASTE RATING •

2

• COMMENTS •

J & B Rare is a smooth, sweet-tasting whisky with a light, fresh character.

Giacomo Justerini, was a wine merchant from Bologna who set up the wine merchants, Justerini and Brooks, in the capital in 1749 and began selling Scotch thirty years later. In 1962 the company built on previous amalgamations by combining with W. & A. Gilbey to form International Distillers and Vintners Ltd (IDV). Grand Metropolitan bought IDV in 1972. J & B Rare is the number two best-selling whisky worldwide.

BLEND

J&B ULTIMA

Justerini & Brooks, London

• STRENGTH •

43%

• TASTE RATING •

3

• COMMENTS •

Ultima has a rich, slightly sweet aroma with a smooth, dry finish.

Giacomo Justerini, was a wine merchant from Bologna who set up the wine merchants, Justerini and Brooks in the capital in 1749 and began selling Scotch thirty years later. The creation this whisky represented the fulfilment of a dream held for many years by J&B's Master Blender, Jim Milne. Ultima is the ultimate blend and a truly unique creation: a blend of 116 malts and 12 grain whiskies, many of which are no longer being produced.

JOHNNIE WALKER BLACK LABEL

United Distillers, Kilmarnock, Ayrshire

• AGE •
12 years

• STRENGTH •
43%

• TASTE RATING •
2–3

• COMMENTS •

The best-selling de luxe Scotch whisky in the world, it has a special quality of smoothness and a depth of taste and character which linger on the palate.

In common with other entrepreneurs who became the major operators in the whisky-blending industry, the original Johnnie Walker began as a licensed grocer in Kilmarnock in 1820. It was his grandsons who created the Black Label and Red Label blends in the early 1900s. His son, Alexander Walker, bought Cardow Distillery in 1893, thus ensuring a regular supply of malt for their blends. In 1925 the company joined the Distillers Company Ltd who bought the Talisker and Dailuaine distilleries and licensed the former to Walker. Johnnie Walker Black Label is now owned by United Distillers.

DELUXE

JOHNNIE WALKER BLUE LABEL

United Distillers, Kilmarnock, Ayrshire

Introduced to the UK market in 1992 under its new name, Blue Label is the latest and most up-market addition to the family of Johnnie Walker 'coloured label' whiskies. Most of the product is intended to go for export, particularly to Japanese markets. The Johnnie Walker company began as a family-run licensed grocers in Kilmarnock in 1820 and by the end of the century had become one of the major players in the Scotch industry. Johnnie Walker is now one of United Distillers' major blending names.

• STRENGTH •

43%

• TASTE RATING •

2-3

• COMMENTS •

Blue Label is among the most exclusive of blended whiskies, with a subtle and complex character and a rich, pleasing flavour.

JOHNNIE WALKER RED LABEL

**United Distillers,
Kilmarnock, Ayrshire**

* STRENGTH *

43%

* TASTE RATING *

2

* COMMENTS *

A smooth blend with sweet and dry notes of maltiness and peatiness. Red Label is the world's biggest-selling blended whisky.

The original Johnnie Walker began as a licensed grocer in Kilmarnock in 1820. It was his grandsons who created the Black Label and Red Label blends in the early 1900s. His son, Alexander Walker, bought Cardow Distillery in 1893, thus ensuring a regular supply of malt for their blends. It was a Walker's employee, James Stevenson, who was instrumental in persuading the government to introduce a minimum period of maturation in bond for whisky, in the process raising quality standards and doing the industry a major service. Johnnie Walker Red Label is now owned by United Distillers.

BLEND

KNOCKANDO

**Knockando Distillery,
Knockando, Aberlour,
Banffshire**

• AGE •

*Bottled when ready, rather
than at a set age; always at
least 12 years.*

• STRENGTH •

40%, 43%

• TASTE RATING •

3-4

• COMMENTS •

*Knockando is a light, easy-to-drink single malt, with
pleasantly smooth, nutty hints.*

• VISITORS •

*Visitors are welcome by
appointment. Telephone
01340-6205 to arrange.*

Built during the 1890s whisky boom, Knockando is today owned by International Distillers and Vintners. Knockando single malt is bottled only when it is considered to have reached its peak rather than at a pre-determined age – generally, this is between twelve and fifteen years. The label lists the year of distillation – the 'season' – and the year of bottling. Such season dating recalls the time when Scottish distilleries only distilled during the winter season after the barley harvest.

LAGAVULIN

**Lagavulin Distillery,
Port Ellen, Islay, Argyll**

• AGE •
16 years

• STRENGTH •
43%

• TASTE RATING •
5

• COMMENTS •
A distinctively Islay malt, powerful and demanding, with a dominant aroma and a dry, peaty–smoky flavour complemented by a trace of sweetness.

• VISITORS •
Visitors are welcome by appointment. Telephone 01496-302400 to arrange.

Distilling was carried on in this area from the 1740s, when moonshiners made and smuggled illicit whisky to the mainland. Lagavulin's own history is entangled with these times, although the distillery dates officially from the 1810s. Peter Mackie, the main driving force behind the success of White Horse, started out on his distilling career at Lagavulin, and its produce was later to feature strongly in his blend. Lagavulin went into partnership with Mackie's company, subsequently the White Horse Company, and the whisky is still used in White Horse blends today. The distillery is owned by United Distillers.

LAPHROAIG

**Laphroaig Distillery,
Port Ellen, Islay, Argyll**

• AGE •

10, 15 years

• STRENGTH •

40%, 43%, up to 45.1%

• TASTE RATING •

5

• COMMENTS •

*A robust, full-bodied, classic
Islay malt with a trace of
seaweed in its strongly peaty
flavour.*

• VISITORS •

*Visitors are welcome by
appointment, Sept.–end June.
Telephone 01496-302418 to
arrange.*

Laphroaig Distillery is set on a bay on Islay's southern shore, and dates back to 1815. It is a traditional distillery and one of the few still to have a hand-turned malting floor. It is owned by Allied Distillers, who consider the single malt, a top-five seller in the world malts list, to be the star performer across their entire portfolio. Laphroaig is also one of the components in their Long John, Ballantine's and Teacher's blends, as well as in the quality Black Bottle blend, which Allied recently sold to Matthew Gloag & Son.

LAUDER'S SCOTCH

Macduff International, Glasgow

- **STRENGTH**

40%, 43%

- **TASTE RATING**

2

- **COMMENTS**

A smooth, nicely rounded and easy-to-drink blend.

- **VISITORS**

The blending and bottling plant is not open to visitors.

The blenders of Lauders, Macduff International, are an independent Scotch whisky company. Lauders has been in continuous production since 1836, making it one of the oldest brands available on the market. Throughout its long history, Lauders has won several gold medals in competition both at home and overseas. As well as Lauders, Macduff International's product range includes the Islay Mist de luxe, as well as the Grand MacNish and Stewart Macduff blends.

BLEND

LEDAIG

SINGLE MALT
FROM
THE ISLE OF MULL

1974
Vintage

This rare old single malt whisky
was distilled at the Ledaig Distillery
on the Isle of Mull by
Ledaig Distillers (Tobermory) Ltd.

PRODUCE OF SCOTLAND

70cl   Sole agent for Switzerland   43%Vol
Jacques Vins et Spiritueux
Jacques Semulovski Geneva

LEDAIG

**Tobermory Distillery,
Tobermory, Mull, Argyll**

● AGE ●

20 years

● STRENGTH ●

43%

● TASTE RATING ●

5

● COMMENTS ●

A full-bodied single malt from the Tobermory Distillery, Ledaig has strongly peaty flavours.

● VISITORS ●

The Visitor Centre and Distillery Shop are open Mon.–Fri., Easter–30 Sept. Tours can be arranged at other times in the year. Telephone 01688-302645.

Tobermory Distillery has enjoyed mixed fortunes since it was first established in 1823. It has been closed several times, most recently in the 1980s. Having reopened in 1989, Tobermory is now back in production and it remains one of the few independent whisky distilleries. The distillery was previously known as Ledaig, changing its name in the 1970s. A single malt is also available under the distillery's new name of Tobermory. The distillery was bought by Burn Stewart Distillers in 1993.

LINKWOOD

**Linkwood Distillery,
Elgin, Moray**

• AGE •

12 years

• STRENGTH •

43%

• TASTE RATING •

4–5

• COMMENTS •

*Linkwood is widely acclaimed
as one of the best Speyside
malts, having the area's characteristics in a fine balance:
smoky, and with a fruity
sweetness underlying its malty
tones.*

• VISITORS •

*Visitors are welcome by
appointment, 0800–1630.
Telephone 01343-547004.*

This is one of the most traditional
of distilleries despite extensive
rebuilding work carried out three
times since its establishment in the
1820s: it is said that equipment was
never replaced until absolutely necessary, and even a spider's web was
not removed in case the change of
environment would affect the
whisky. Built by a former provost of
Elgin, Linkwood has an attractive
wooded setting by Linkwood Burn
outside the town. The distillery is
owned by United Distillers.

PRODUCT OF SCOTLAND

LITTLEMILL

Established 1772

SINGLE LOWLAND MALT
SCOTCH WHISKY

DISTILLED AND BOTTLED IN SCOTLAND BY

LITTLEMILL DISTILLERY CO. LTD.
BOWLING, DUNBARTONSHIRE, SCOTLAND

70cl ℮   40%vol

LITTLEMILL

**Littlemill Distillery, Bowling,
Dunbartonshire**

• AGE •

8 years

• STRENGTH •

40%

• TASTE RATING •

2-3

• COMMENTS •

*A light Lowland malt with a
smooth, sweet flavour. Good
as an aperitif.*

• VISITORS •

*The distillery is not open to the
public.*

L ittlemill began life as a brewery
centuries before distilling was
started, with its ale apparently crossing the Clyde to supply the monks of
Paisley Abbey. It was established as
a distillery in the late eighteenth century and is one of the oldest in
Scotland. Its water comes from the
Kilpatrick Hills, to the north of the
Highland Line, although Littlemill is
a Lowland distillery and whisky.
Since 1994, it ha been under the
control of the Loch Lomond
Distillery Co., the producers of
Inchmurrin single malt. Littlemill is
presently mothballed.

THE LOCH FYNE

**Loch Fyne Whiskies,
Inveraray, Argyll**

● STRENGTH ●

40%

● TASTE RATING ●

2–3

● COMMENTS ●

*A malt drinker's blend, full
flavoured, with a raisiny,
sweet spiced nose, mellow
smoothness of taste and a
warming finish. A very easy-
to-drink whisky.*

● VISITORS ●

*The shop is open all year,
1000–1730 (except Sun.,
Nov.–Mar.). Telephone 01499-
302219 for mail-order
information.*

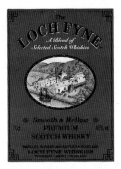

Loch Fyne Whiskies is an independent specialist shop devoted to selling only whisky and whisky-related products. First registered in 1884, the current Loch Fyne blend was created by Ronnie Martin, a former production director of DCL/United Distillers. His mastery of blending was recognised when in 1996, The Loch Fyne won the bronze award in the influential International Wine & Spirit Competition. Produced in small quantities, it is available only in Argyll or by mail-order.

BLEND

LOCH RANZA

Isle of Arran Distillers Ltd, Mauchline, Ayrshire

• STRENGTH •

40%

• TASTE RATING •

2

• COMMENTS •

Clean, fresh and medium-dry, this blend betrays its provenance, showing aromas of the sea and pinewoods with a light floral note to the peatiness.

Isle of Arran Distillers are a dynamic new player in the Scotch whisky industry. Independent and family-run, the company has a portfolio of blended and malt whiskies which has been successfully marketed throughout Europe, the Americas and Asia. In 1995, the company opened a new distillery on Arran at Lochranza and its first produce is presently maturing, with an expected launch as a single malt early in the new millennium.

LOCHSIDE

**Lochside Distillery,
Montrose, Angus**

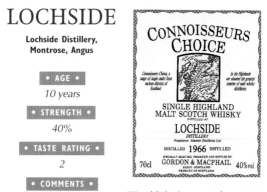

• AGE •
10 years

• STRENGTH •
40%

• TASTE RATING •
2

• COMMENTS •

A light-to-medium-bodied single malt with a sweet, fruity aroma and drier, smooth flavour. It is difficult to find under the distillery label, but supplies will continue to be available from independent merchants.

Established as recently as 1957, Lochside has been one of the shorter-lived Scotch whisky distilleries. It was built on the site of an eighteenth-century brewery and originally comprised two distilleries, one grain and one malt, as well as a blending plant. The distillery closed its grain-distilling and blending facilities in the late 1970s and continued in malt production only until 1992, when it was shut down completely by its Spanish owners.

LONG JOHN

Allied Distillers, Dumbarton, Dunbartonshire

● STRENGTH ●

40%, 43%

● TASTE RATING ●

2-3

● COMMENTS ●

A medium-bodied blend with a very slight peaty tang to its pleasant, nicely rounded flavour.

● VISITORS ●

The plant is not suitable for visitors.

The original company was found-ed by 'Long' John Macdonald, a statuesque man who built Ben Nevis Distillery at Fort William in 1825. The distillery had grain and malt stills, and its produce changed from a malt to a blend around the turn of the century. The Long John company name and the distillery went separate ways, and after passing through several hands and a company name change to Long John International in 1971, is now operated by Allied Distillers.

LONGMORN

**Longmorn Distillery,
Elgin, Moray**

The distillery was built by John
Duff in 1894 and stands on the
road between Elgin and Rothes.
Nearby is an old water wheel dating from the seventeenth century,
although the distillery draws its water
from a local spring. Longmorn, along
with its sister distillery of Benriach,
merged with The Glenlivet and Glen
Grant Distilleries and Hill Thomson
to form The Glenlivet Distillers. The
distillery at that time was known as
Longmorn-Glenlivet, but has now
dropped its hyphenated suffix. The
company was purchased by
Seagram in 1976.

LONGROW

**Springbank Distillery,
Campbeltown, Argyll**

• AGE •

21 years

• STRENGTH •

46%

• TASTE RATING •

5

• COMMENTS •

*Longrow is a pungent malt
whose production process,
using only peat-dried barley,
lends it a distinctive, peaty taste
with an almost medicinal
aroma, yet a complementary
trace of sweetness.*

• VISITORS •

*Springbank Distillery is open to
visitors strictly by appointment.
Telephone 01586-552085 to
arrange.*

Springbank Distillery produces
Longrow as its second malt. It is
called after another Campbeltown
distillery of that name, which was
closed in the late 1800s. Springbank
is a unique for several reasons: it is
the only distillery-label malt which
follows traditional techniques of not
chill-filtering; it is the only distillery
to carry out all production techniques, from floor malting to bottling
itself; it is the only distillery in
Campbeltown not to have closed;
and it has been owned by the same
family for close on two centuries.

THE MACALLAN

Macallan Distillery, Craigellachie, Banffshire

• AGE •

7, 10, 12, 18, 25 years

• STRENGTH •

40%, 43%, 57%

• TASTE RATING •

3–4

• COMMENTS •

Its rich, sherried aroma with a hint of peaches, its smooth, elegant flavour and its delightfully mellow aftertaste make the Macallan one of the most popular of malts.

• VISITORS •

Visitors are welcome by appointment on weekdays. Telephone 01340-871471.

PRODUCE OF SCOTLAND

ESTABLISHED 1824

The **MACALLAN**

Single Highland Malt Scotch Whisky

YEARS **12** OLD

DISTILLED AND BOTTLED BY

THE MACALLAN DISTILLERS LTD
CRAIGELLACHIE SCOTLAND

43% vol   700 ml

The Macallan's distinctive richness of taste and colour derives in part from its ageing in sweet sherry casks, a traditional practice which this distillery is the only one to maintain through all its range. The distillery itself originated on a farm set above a ford over the River Spey, with the first licensed distilling taking place around 1824. It was bought and extended in 1892 by Roderick Kemp, whose descendants owned the company until it was acquired by Highland Distilleries in 1996.

SINGLE MALT

MILLBURN

**Millburn Distillery,
Inverness, Inverness-shire**

• AGE •

varies

• STRENGTH •

varies

• TASTE RATING •

3-4

• COMMENTS •

A rich Highland malt of medium-to-full body with a certain fruitiness in the palate and a balancing dry finish. Available from independent merchants.

Millburn was one of three Inverness distilleries (the others being Glen Albyn and Glen Mhor), none of which is still in existence, Millburn itself having been closed in 1985 and later sold off by its owners, United Distillers. It was also one of the older Highland distilleries, having been established around 1825, although distilling was said to have been carried out on the site as early as 1807. All its produce was traditionally used for blending, so it is difficult to find as a single and its malt will, of course, become rarer in future.

MILTONDUFF

**Miltonduff-Glenlivet
Distillery, Elgin, Moray**

• AGE •
12 years

• STRENGTH •
40%, 43%

• TASTE RATING •
2–3

• COMMENTS •
A nice Speyside malt, medium-bodied and smooth, with a floral note.

• VISITORS •
Visitors are welcome by appointment. Telephone 01343-547433 to arrange.

Miltonduff-Glenlivet Distillery stands just to the south of Elgin near Pluscarden Abbey; the distillery's old mashhouse was said to have been built on the site of the abbey's brewery. The distillery itself was founded in 1824, and draws its water from the nearby Black Burn which flows down peaty Black Hill. Miltonduff was one of the original Hiram Walker distilleries acquired in 1937 and today is operated by Allied Distillers who use it in their blends, notably Ballantine's.

SINGLE MALT

MORTLACH

**Mortlach Distillery,
Dufftown, Keith, Banffshire**

● AGE ●

16 years

● STRENGTH ●

43%

● TASTE RATING ●

4

● COMMENTS ●

*A Speyside malt of mellow,
fruity flavour with a definite
peatiness and a dryness in the
finish.*

● VISITORS ●

*Visitors are welcome by
appointment. Telephone
01340-820318 to arrange.*

Another of Dufftown's distilleries, this time standing in a little valley outside the town, by the River Dullan. The distillery draws its water not from the river but from springs in the local Conval Hills. Founded in 1823, it was, in fact, the first of the distilleries to be built in the capital of Speyside whisky-making, and it enjoyed a monopoly in the town until 1887. The distillery has been modernized twice this century and is now owned by United Distillers, who did not officially bottle its malt until the 1990s.

NORTH PORT

**North Port Distillery,
Brechin, Angus**

● AGE ●

varies

● STRENGTH ●

varies

● TASTE RATING ●

2

● COMMENTS ●

*Available from independent
bottling merchants, North Port
is a light-bodied, dry, fairly
astringent whisky, best drunk
as an aperitif.*

The older of the two distilleries in
Brechin (Glencadam being the
other), North Port was founded in
1820 by David Guthrie, a prominent
Brechin businessman and local
politician, and managed by his sons
from 1823; two brothers in the
Guthrie family had interests in the
whisky industry while a third,
Thomas, was active in the
temperance movement. The
distillery, latterly owned by the
Distillers Company Ltd, was closed
down in 1983 and sold in 1990.

SINGLE MALT

OBAN

**Oban Distillery,
Oban, Argyll**

● AGE ●

14 years

● STRENGTH ●

43%

● TASTE RATING ●

2-3

● COMMENTS ●

*An intriguing, complex malt
with a full Island character
which is balanced by a soft
Highland finish.*

● VISITORS ●

*Visitors are welcome
0930–1700 Mon.–Fri. all year
and 0930–1700 Sat., Easter–
Oct. Telephone 01631-62110.*

F irst built as a brewery in 1794,
Oban Distillery was part of the
grand plan of the Stevensons, a
family of energetic entrepreneurs
and the founders of modern Oban at
that time. The distillery, a grey building standing on the harbour front,
draws its water from the Ardconnel
area of peaty hills a mile from the
town. It is licensed to John Hopkins,
now owned by United Distillers,
who currently feature the single in
their Classic Malts series.

OLD FETTERCAIRN

**Fettercairn Distillery,
Fettercairn, Kincardineshire**

• AGE •
10 years

• STRENGTH •
40%, 43%

• TASTE RATING •
3–4

• COMMENTS •

A smooth single malt with a full, malty taste and a satisfyingly dry counterbalance.

• VISITORS •

Visitors are welcome at the distillery's visitor centre 1000–1630 Mon.–Sat., May–Sept. Telephone 01561-340205 to arrange group bookings.

First established at its present location in 1824, Fettercairn is one of the country's oldest distilleries. Despite its age, it proved receptive to modern production methods when it became the first distillery in the country to use oil for heating its stills. It was once owned by John Gladstone, the father of the great Victorian prime minister W. E. Gladstone. The distillery, which was extended in 1966, is presently owned by Whyte & Mackay.

SINGLE MALT

OLD PARR

**United Distillers,
Banbeath, Leven, Fife**

• AGE •

12 years

• STRENGTH •

43%

• TASTE RATING •

2

• COMMENTS •

A blend of fine whiskies, with a smooth and mellow taste and exceptional depth of flavour.

The firm which produced Old Parr, Macdonald Greenlees, is now owned by United Distillers. The brand was first produced in the early twentieth century by the Greenlees brothers from Glasgow, and was aimed specifically at the southern English market. After the First World War, the company amalgamated with Alexander & Macdonald of Leith and William Williams of Aberdeen, owners of Glendullan Distillery. The whole company joined the Distillers Company Ltd in 1925. Old Parr is a major export blend in Central and South American, Japan and the Far Eastern markets.

OLD PULTENEY

**Pulteney Distillery,
Wick, Caithness**

• AGE •

12 years

• STRENGTH •

40%

• TASTE RATING •

3–4

• COMMENTS •

Reputedly one of the fastest-maturing whiskies, Old Pulteney is a distinctive malt with a pungent aroma and salty tang underlain by peaty notes, perhaps due to the exposed coastal position of the distillery. Available from independent bottlers.

• VISITORS •

The distillery is not open to visitors.

Pulteney Distillery was established in 1826 in a new district of Wick which had been built to accommodate workers from the local herring industry, and in such a situation it had a ready market. It was closed during the slump of the 1920s and was not reopened until 1951. In June 1995 the distillery was sold by Allied Distillers to Inver House Distillers, giving them a complement of four malt distilleries, the others being Knockdhu, Speyburn-Glenlivet and, most recently, Balblair. Pulteney is the most northerly distillery on the Scottish mainland.

SINGLE MALT

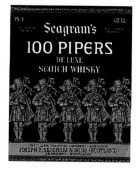

100 PIPERS

**Chivas Brothers,
Paisley**

A smooth, mellow blend with a light, smoky finish.

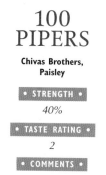

Chivas Brothers is a subsidiary of the Canadian drinks firm Seagram, by whom it was bought in 1949. The origins of the Chivas Brothers company can be traced back to the establishment of a wine and spirit merchant and licensed grocer in Aberdeen in 1801. As the owner of nine distilleries, Seagram is an important company in the Scotch whisky market. 100 Pipers is one of several Seagram-owned blended whiskies, among which Passport and the de luxe Chivas Regal and Royal Salute are especially well regarded.

BLEND

THE ORIGINAL MACKINLAY

Invergordon Distillers, Leith, Edinburgh

The success of the Mackinlay firm began under James, son of Charles Mackinlay, founder of the Leith company in 1824. The original Mackinlay's blend appeared in 1850, and James was responsible for its success in the lucrative markets of southern England, gaining contracts to supply whisky to the House of Commons and to Ernest Shackleton's 1907 expedition to the South Pole. The company is now owned by Whyte & Mackay.

BLEND

PASSPORT

**Chivas Brothers,
Paisley**

• STRENGTH •

40%

• TASTE RATING •

2-3

• COMMENTS •

*A well-rounded blend which
has the Glen Keith single malt
at its core. Sweet, slighty fruity
flavours are complemented by
a delicate smoky finish.*

Chivas Brothers is a subsidiary of
the Canadian drinks firm
Seagram, by whom it was bought
in 1949. The origins of the Chivas
Brothers company can be traced
back to the establishment of a wine
and spirit merchant and licensed
grocer in Aberdeen in 1801.
Owning nine malt distilleries,
Seagram is an important company in
the Scotch whisky market. Passport
was launched in 1965 after several
years' research to produce a blend
that would appeal specifically to a
younger, less traditional market.

PINWINNIE

Inver House Distillers, Moffat Distillery, Airdrie, Lanarkshire

• STRENGTH •

40%

• TASTE RATING •

2–3

• COMMENTS •

A Lowland de luxe blend, Pinwinnie is a very smooth whisky, with sweet, fragrant notes and a nicely rounded finish.

• VISITORS •

The distillery and plant are not open to visitors.

Pinwinnie's producers, Inver House, also own Knockdhu (producing An Cnoc single malt) and Speyburn-Glenlivet distilleries, and have also recently acquired Pulteney and Balblair. Since a management buy-out from its parent company, Publicker Distillers, in 1988, Inver House has been one of the few independent, Scottish-owned companies in the whisky industry. Blending is carried out at their complex at Moffat on the outskirts of Airdrie in the central Lowlands, a converted former paper mill.

PITTYVAICH

Pittyvaich-Glenlivet Distillery, Dufftown, Keith, Banffshire

SINGLE MALT
SCOTCH WHISKY

PITTYVAICH

Distillery is situated in the DULLAN GLEN on the outskirts of Dufftown, near to the historic Mortlach Church which dates back to the 6th. The distillery draws water from two nearby

springs CONVALLEYS and BALLIEMORE Pittyvaich single MALT SCOTCH WHISKY has a perfumed, fruity nose and a robust flavour with a hint of spiciness.

AGED 12 YEARS

43% vol 70cl

* **AGE** *
12 years

* **STRENGTH** *
43%

* **TASTE RATING** *
4

* **COMMENTS** *

Pittyvaich is a Speyside malt with a perfumed fruitiness with a hint of spice and a strong aftertaste.

It was the success of neighbouring Dufftown-Glenlivet and the quality of its water supply, from the local Jock's Well, which encouraged Bell to build the brand-new Pittyvaich-Glenlivet Distillery almost next door, in 1974. Almost all of its product now goes into United Distillers' blends, and the single malt was difficult to find until it was officially bottled by UD as part of their Distillery (Flora and Fauna) Malts series. The distillery has now been closed.

PORT ELLEN

**Port Ellen Distillery,
Port Ellen, Islay, Argyll**

• AGE •
varies

• STRENGTH •
varies

• TASTE RATING •
3–4

• COMMENTS •

A milder Islay than some, Port Ellen is a basically dry malt with a reasonably mild, smoky and peaty flavour. It is available from independent bottling merchants.

Port Ellen was established in 1824 and stands in the town of the same name in the south of the island. The distillery was closed earlier this century, from 1930 until 1967, when it was re-opened, modernized and enlarged. Its produce has been regarded by some conoisseurs as the classic Islay malt. The distillery, latterly owned by United Distillers, was mothballed in 1984 and has now been closed permanently.

SINGLE MALT

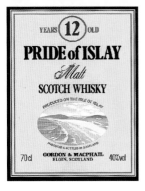

PRIDE OF ISLAY

Gordon and MacPhail, Elgin, Moray

• AGE •

12 years

• STRENGTH •

40%

• TASTE RATING •

4

• COMMENTS •

One of Gordon and MacPhail's series of malts capturing the classic characteristics of the leading regions, this is a vatting of the finest Islay whiskies. It has a complex nose with salty, medicinal and smoky flavours.

• VISITORS •

Gordon and MacPhail's shop, South St, Elgin is open 0900–1715 Mon.–Wed. (0900–1300 Wed. in winter.), 0830–1715 Thu.–Fri., 0900–1700 Sat.

Gordon and MacPhail started in business in 1895 as a licensed grocers and wine and spirit merchant, as had done so many of the foremost names among the Scotch whisky blending industry. Unlike the others, however, Gordon and MacPhail have retained all the original aspects of their business as well as extending into vatting, blending and bottling, and they are today the world's leading malt whisky specialists.

PRIDE OF THE LOWLANDS

Gordon and MacPhail, Elgin, Moray

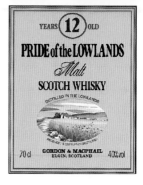

• AGE •
12 years

• STRENGTH •
40%

• TASTE RATING •
2

• COMMENTS •
One of Gordon and MacPhail's series of malts capturing the classic characteristics of the leading regions, this is a vatting of the finest Lowland whiskies, and has a sweet, butterscotch-like nose with a smoky–woody finish.

• VISITORS •
Gordon and MacPhail's shop, South St, Elgin is open 0900–1715 Mon.–Wed. (0900–1300 Wed. in winter.), 0830–1715 Thu.–Fri., 0900–1700 Sat.

Gordon and MacPhail's premises are located in Elgin on the banks of the River Lossie and close to Speyside, arguably the heart of the Scotch whisky industry. The firm has been in business for almost a century, initially as a licensed grocers and wine and spirit merchants. Their business encompasses the vatting, blending and bottling of whiskies, while their retail shop is among the leading malt whisky shops in the UK.

PRIDE OF ORKNEY

Gordon and MacPhail, Elgin, Moray

• AGE •

12 years

• STRENGTH •

40%, 43%, 57%

• TASTE RATING •

3

• COMMENTS •

One of Gordon and MacPhail's series of malts capturing the classic characteristics of the leading regions, this is a vatting of the finest whiskies produced in Orkney, and is a well-balanced whisky with a sweet, toasted nose, with a hint of heather.

• VISITORS •

Gordon and MacPhail's shop, South St, Elgin is open 0900–1715 Mon.–Wed. (0900–1300 Wed. in winter.), 0830–1715 Thu.–Fri., 0900–1700 Sat.

Gordon and MacPhail started in business in 1895 as a licensed grocers and wine and spirit merchant, as had done so many of the foremost names among the Scotch whisky blending industry. Unlike the others, however, Gordon and MacPhail have retained all the original aspects of their business as well as extending into vatting, blending and bottling, and they are today the world's leading malt whisky specialists.

PRIDE OF STRATHSPEY

Gordon and MacPhail, Elgin, Moray

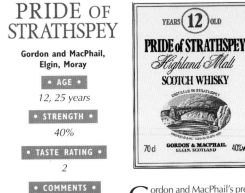

* COMMENTS *

One of Gordon and MacPhail's series of malts capturing the classic characteristics of the leading regions, this is a vatting of the finest Strathspey whiskies. This malt is a citrus-fruity whisky in nose and palate, with a very pleasant aftertaste.

* VISITORS *

Gordon and MacPhail's shop, South St, Elgin is open 0900–1715 Mon.–Wed. (0900–1300 Wed. in winter.), 0830–1715 Thu.–Fri., 0900–1700 Sat.

Gordon and MacPhail's premises are located in Elgin on the banks of the River Lossie and close to Speyside, arguably the heart of the Scotch whisky industry. The firm has been in business for almost a century, initially as a licensed grocers and wine and spirit merchants. Their business encompasses the vatting, blending and bottling of whiskies, while their retail shop is among the leading malt whisky shops in the UK.

ROSEBANK

**Rosebank Distillery,
Camelon, Falkirk,
Stirlingshire**

• AGE •
12 years

• STRENGTH •
43%

• TASTE RATING •
2

• COMMENTS •

*One of the best known
Lowland malts, Rosebank is a
smooth, mild whisky of light
and subtle character, which
makes it ideal as a pre-dinner
dram.*

Although a distillery was operating on this site in 1817, the most recent distillery generally dated from 1840, when much rebuilding took place. It stands on the banks of the Forth and Clyde Canal, on the outskirts of Falkirk. Triple distillation processes were used at Rosebank, which had one wash still and two spirit stills. The distillery is now closed.

ROYAL BRACKLA

Royal Brackla Distillery, Cawdor, Nairnshire

10 years

43%

4

A light, fresh, grassy malt with a hint of fruitiness. This single malt can be difficult to find.

Visitors are welcome by appointment. Telephone 016677-404280.

While William IV was known to have enjoyed Brackla's whisky, the distillery has been allowed officially to call itself 'Royal' since 1838, when his neice, the new queen Victoria granted it a Royal Warrant. Founded in 1812, the distillery has been rebuilt and extended several times in the past two centuries, although it is currently mothballed. It is licensed to Bissets, now owned by United Distillers, and almost all of its produce goes into their blends.

SINGLE MALT

ROYAL CULROSS

Gibson Scotch Whisky Distilleries Ltd, Glasgow

• AGE •
8 years

• STRENGTH •
43%

• TASTE RATING •
3-4

• COMMENTS •

Royal Culross is a vatted malt of substantial character and body with a pungent aroma and smooth, malty tones balanced by a lighter, slightly peaty edge.

Royal Culross is one of a range of whiskies, including the popular blend Fraser McDonald and Scotia Royale de luxe blend, which are associated with the Glen Scotia Distillery in Campbeltown. All three are produced by Gibson Scotch Whisky Distilleries Ltd, a subsidiary of the Loch Lomond Distillery Co. Ltd of Alexandria. The company now has three malt distilleries (Loch Lomond which produces Inchmurrin, a Highland malt, Littlemill, a Lowland malt, and Glen Scotia from Campbeltown) as well as one grain distillery on the site at Alexandria.

ROYAL LOCHNAGAR

**Royal Lochnagar Distillery,
Crathie, Ballater,
Aberdeenshire**

AGE

12 years

STRENGTH

40%

TASTE RATING

3–4

COMMENTS

*A big-bodied, rich and highly
fruity malt with a delightfully
sherried flavour.*

VISITORS

*Visitors are welcome
1000–1700 Mon.–Fri. all year.
Telephone 01339-742273.*

Lochnagar Distillery was built in 1826 by James Robertson, an infamous local illicit distiller. Distilling was not peaceful work at that time: Lochnagar was destroyed by fire, reputedly the work of rival illicit distillers, in 1841 before being taken over and rebuilt by John Begg four years later. Its 'Royal' prefix came after a visit and tasting in 1848 by Queen Victoria (said to be partial to whisky) and Prince Albert, who were staying at nearby Balmoral. The distillery was bought by Dewar and is now owned by United Distillers.

SINGLE MALT

ST MAGDALENE

St Magdalene Distillery, Linlithgow, West Lothian

• AGE •
varies

• STRENGTH •
varies

• TASTE RATING •
2-3

| • COMMENTS • |

A light-bodied Lowland malt, smooth and generally dry yet with a hint of fruity sweetness. Available only from independent merchants and their retail outlets, its produce can be difficult to find.

St Magdalene, built on the lands of St Mary's Cross towards the end of the nineteenth century, was until recently the sole survivor of the six distilleries which existed in Linlithgow in the last century. All the distillery's production officially went into blends, although it is still available through independent bottlers. St Magdalene was closed by its owners, United Distillers, in the mid 1980s, with the building subsequently being converted to private housing.

SCAPA

**Scapa Distillery,
Kirkwall, Orkney**

- **AGE** •

12 years

- **STRENGTH** •

40%

- **TASTE RATING** •

3

- **COMMENTS** •

Scapa is a medium-bodied malt with a dryish, heathery flavour which is complemented by a satisfyingly malty sweetness.

- **VISITORS** •

The distillery has no reception centre, but visitors are welcome by appointment. Telephone 01856-872071 to arrange.

Scapa is one of two distilleries in Kirkwall (Highland Park being the other), yet despite their proximity, their whiskies taste quite different. Scapa was built in 1885 by Macfarlane and Townsend – the latter already a well-known distiller on Speyside – and was bought by Hiram Walker in 1954. It is now owned by Allied Distillers who send most of its produce for blending, but also market the single largely through duty-free outlets.

SCOTIA ROYALE

Gibson Scotch Whisky Distilleries Ltd, Glasgow

• AGE •

12 years

• STRENGTH •

40%, 43%

• TASTE RATING •

2-3

• COMMENTS •

A medium-bodied de luxe blend, Scotia Royale is a smooth, well-balanced whisky with a hint of peat. Glen Scotia malt is one of this whisky's most important ingredients.

Scotia Royale is one of a range of whiskies, including the popular blend Fraser McDonald and Royal Culross vatted malt, which are associated with the Glen Scotia Distillery in Campbeltown. All three are produced by Gibson Scotch Whisky Distilleries Ltd, a subsidiary of the Loch Lomond Distillery Co. Ltd of Alexandria. The company now has three malt distilleries (Loch Lomond which produces Inchmurrin, a Highland malt, Littlemill, a Lowland malt, and Glen Scotia from Campbeltown) as well as one grain distillery on the site at Alexandria.

THE SINGLETON OF AUCHROISK

Auchroisk Distillery, Mulben, Banffshire

AGED 10 YEARS

• AGE •

minimum 10 years

• STRENGTH •

40%

• TASTE RATING •

2–3

• COMMENTS •

This whisky is medium-bodied, with a hint of peat to its flavour, which is smooth and sweet, derived from part-maturation in sherry casks.

• VISITORS •

Visitors are welcome by appointment on weekdays. Telephone 01542-8606333 to arrange.

One of the newest Scots whisky distilleries (opened in 1974), Auchroisk was built by International Distillers and Vintners and is licensed to Justerini & Brooks. Dorie's Well provides the distillery with its pure, natural water source. The building itself has won several awards, including one from the Angling Foundation for not interfering with the progress of local salmon as they swim upriver. The company has been marketing its single malt since 1987 but it is already a winner of twelve major awards.

SINGLE MALT

SPEYBURN

**Speyburn-Glenlivet
Distillery, Rothes, Moray**

10 years

40%

3-4

*A medium-bodied whisky with
a firm yet subtle flavour and a
dry, warming, peaty finish.*

*The distillery is not open to
visitors.*

Speyburn was built in 1897 on the outskirts of Rothes, and outwardly has hardly been altered in the past century. Set among rolling green slopes, it is one of the most picturesque distilleries in Scotland. It was originally built for the blenders John Hopkins and later acquired by United Distillers. Its produce was difficult to find as a single malt until it was bought from UD in 1992 by the independent Inver House Distillers.

SPRINGBANK

**Springbank Distillery,
Campbelltown, Argyll**

• AGE •

12, 15, 21, 25 years

• STRENGTH •

46%, 57%

• TASTE RATING •

4

• COMMENTS •

*Often described as a classic
malt, Springbank is a smooth,
mellow whisky, light yet complex and full-flavoured.*

• VISITORS •

*The distillery is open to visi-
tors strictly by appointment.
Telephone 01586-552085 to
arrange.*

Springbank was built in 1828 by
the Mitchell family, previous
owners of an illicit still in the area.
The distillery is still owned today by
the founders' family, and has never
been closed at any time in its history.
Along with Glenfiddich, Springbank
is unusual in bottling on the
premises, and is also the only
Scottish distillery to carry out the full
malt whisky production process.
Springbank is not coloured with
caramel, and is the only malt sold
under a distillery label which has not
been chill-filtered. Longrow single
malt is also produced here.

STAG'S BREATH LIQUEUR

Meikles of Scotland, Newtonmore, Inverness-shire

● STRENGTH ●

19.8%

● TASTE RATING ●

2

● COMMENTS ●

M eikles of Scotland is a small Speyside family firm and has been producing Stag's Breath since 1989. The liqueur takes its name from one of the fictional whiskies lost at sea in Sir Compton Mackenzie's famous re-telling of the wartime sinking of the SS *Politician*, in his book, *Whisky Galore*.

A light and smooth union of fine Speyside whisky with heather comb honey. Equally suited to a role as an aperitif or as a digestif.

● VISITORS ●

Meikles have no visitor facilities at present.

STEWART MACDUFF

Macduff International, Glasgow

43% vol   **75 cl**

• AGE •
12 years

• STRENGTH •
40%, 43%

• TASTE RATING •
2

• COMMENTS •

A smooth, medium-bodied blend of Highland, Islay and Lowland malts with mildly peaty overtones.

• VISITORS •

The blending and bottling plant is not open to visitors.

Stewart Macduff is a relative newcomer to the range of whiskies produced by Macduff International Ltd, an independent Scotch whisky company. As well as this blend, the company's portfolio includes the de luxe Islay Mist blend and Lauders, one of the oldest brands of Scotch on the market, as well as the Grand MacNish and Strathbeag blends.

BLEND

STEWARTS CREAM OF THE BARLEY

**Allied Distillers,
Dumbarton, Dunbartonshire**

STRENGTH

40%

TASTE RATING

2

COMMENTS

A popular and good-quality blend with a soft and well-balanced, sweetish, malty flavour.

VISITORS

The plant is not suitable for visitors.

Stewart & Son of Dundee was founded in 1831 and was one of the first companies to exploit newer methods of distilling, particularly the new patent still, and the beginnings of the market for blended whiskies. The company grew steadily in size and the brand in popularity. It was bought by Allied-Lyons in 1969 and today operates under Allied Distillers as one of their most popular standard blends for the UK market.

STRATHISLA

**Strathisla Distillery,
Keith, Banffshire**

• AGE •
12 years

• STRENGTH •
43%

• TASTE RATING •
4

• COMMENTS •
A big, robust whisky which is full-flavoured and fruity, with a nutty, sherried sweetness.

• VISITORS •
Visitors are welcome 0930–1600 Mon.–Fri., Feb.-mid March and Nov., 0930–1600 Mon.-Sat.and Sun. 1230-1600, mid March to end Oct.. Telephone 01542-783042.

According to records, production of a 'heather ale' by local clerics had been taking place in this area as early as 1208. The later siting of Milton Distillery (as Strathisla was formerly known) here in the eighteenth century may have been for the same reasons: set in a good barley-producing area, with easy access to a pure local spring which had been a holy well of local Cistercian monks, and said to be guarded by water spirits. The distillery was bought by Chivas Brothers, a Seagram subsidiary, in 1950.

SINGLE MALT

ISLE OF SKYE
TALISKER
SINGLE MALT SCOTCH WHISKY

45.8% vol   TALISKER DISTILLERY CARBOST AKTS   1 Litre ℮

TALISKER

**Talisker Distillery,
Carbost, Isle of Skye**

• AGE •
8, 10 years

• STRENGTH •
45.8%

• TASTE RATING •
5

• COMMENTS •
Talisker is Skye's only malt and has been described as being mid-way between Islay and Highland malts. It is full-bodied with a rich, peaty flavour and elements of malty, fruity sweetness.

• VISITORS •
Visitors are welcome 0930–1630 Mon.–Fri., Apr.–Oct., and by appointment 1400–1630 Nov.– Mar. Telephone 0147-842203.

Talisker Distillery had an inauspicious start in the 1830s, being denounced by a local minister as a great curse for the area. Despite his disapproval, distilling has continued successfully, with the distillery changing hands several times. A victim of several fires throughout its 160-year history, it was almost completely rebuilt in 1960. The distillery is owned today by United Distillers, and some of its product goes into Johnnie Walker blends. The single malt was even praised by Robert Louis Stevenson in his poem, *The Scotsman's Return from Abroad*, as one of 'The King o' drinks'.

SINGLE MALT

TAMDHU

**Tamdhu Distillery,
Knockando, Aberlour,
Banffshire**

• AGE •

no age given

• STRENGTH •

40%, 43%

• TASTE RATING •

3

• COMMENTS •

*A good, light-to-medium
Speyside malt, which is
slightly peaty but with a
delicate sweetness and a long,
subtle finish.*

• VISITORS •

*The distillery is not open to
visitors.*

FINE SINGLE MALT
BOTTLED IN SCOTLAND
ESTD 1897
MALTED AND DISTILLED AT
TAMDHU DISTILLERY
SPEYSIDE SCOTLAND
*water from our own spring,
our own malted barley,
and a full barrow loads of peat*
PRODUCT OF SCOTLAND
SCOTCH WHISKY

Highland Distilleries bought this distillery shortly after it opened in 1897 and have owned it ever since. It was extensively refurbished in the 1970s and is now one of the most modern distilleries on Speyside. Set in the Spey valley, Tamdhu used to favour the hyphenated Glenlivet suffix, but this has been dropped in recent years. As well as its appearance as a single malt, Tamdhu features in The Famous Grouse blend, owned by Highland's subsidiary, Matthew Gloag & Son.

TAMNAVULIN

**Tamnavulin Distillery,
Tomnavoulin, Banffshire**

● AGE ●
10, 26 years

● STRENGTH ●
40%

● TASTE RATING ●
3

● COMMENTS ●

A lightish, mellow Glenlivet-type malt with a sweetish bouquet and taste but an underlying grapey note.

Opened in 1966, this was one of the newest Highland distilleries. A rather functional building, it is set on slopes above the River Livet and used water from a nearby burn. This is another distillery which once carried the hyphenated Glenlivet suffix but has since shed it. Tamnavulin was owned until 1993 by Invergordon Distillers, but Whyte & Mackay acquired the group that year. Since then production has been mothballed here and at two of the other former Invergordon malt distilleries, Tullibardine and Bruichladdich.

TEACHER'S HIGHLAND CREAM

**Allied Distillers,
Dumbarton, Dunbartonshire**

• STRENGTH •

40%, 43%

• TASTE RATING •

2

• COMMENTS •

*Teacher's Highland Cream is a
superior blend which has a
smooth, sweet flavour with a
trace of dryer, heathery notes.
It is one of the most popular
blended whiskies in the UK.
Its sister blend is the 12-year-
old Teacher's Royal Highland.*

• VISITORS •

*The plant is not suitable for
visitors.*

The Teacher's company was
begun in Glasgow in the 1830s
by William Teacher, a young man
barely in his twenties. The business
started with licensed premises and
expanded to include blending, bottling and export interests. Highland
Cream was first marketed in 1884,
although Teacher's did not build its
first distillery, at Ardmore, until 1898.
The company later sold off its
licensed shops. Today the company
is owned by Allied Distillers and the
blend sells into 150 countries.

BLEND

TEANINICH

**Teaninich Distillery,
Alness, Ross-shire**

• AGE •

10 years

• STRENGTH •

43%

• TASTE RATING •

3

• COMMENTS •

A difficult-to-find single malt, Teaninich is assertive with a spicy, smoky and satisfying taste.

• VISITORS •

Visitors are welcome by appointment only. Telephone 01349-882461 to arrange.

Teaninich Distillery dates from the early 1800s and in 1887 it was recorded as the only distillery north of Inverness to be 'lighted by electricity'. The majority of the present buildings date from the 1970s and it is now owned by United Distillers who reopened it in 1990 after it was mothballed for several years. Most of the production has traditionally gone into blending, but the single malt has become easier to find since its official bottling as part of UD's Distillery (Flora and Fauna) Malts series.

TOBERMORY

Tobermory Distillery, Tobermory, Isle of Mull

• AGE •

no age given

• STRENGTH •

40%

• TASTE RATING •

3

• COMMENTS •

A nicely balanced, light malt with a delicate, flowery aroma and drier, heathery tones in its flavour. A good pre-dinner dram.

• VISITORS •

The Visitor Centre and Distillery Shop are open Mon.– Fri., Easter–30 Sept. Tours can be arranged at other times in the year. Telephone 01688-302645.

Set in a wooded site by the sea, Tobermory Distillery has enjoyed mixed fortunes since it was first established in 1823. It has been closed several times during its existence, most recently in the 1980s when it was mothballed. Having reopened in 1989, the distillery is now back in production. The distillery was previously known as Ledaig but changed its name in the 1970s; a single malt marketed under the old name is available. Tobermory remains one of the few independent distilleries. It was bought by Burn Stewart Distillers in 1993.

TOMATIN

**Tomatin Distillery,
Tomatin, Inverness-shire**

• AGE •
10, 12, 25 years

• STRENGTH •
40%, 43%

• TASTE RATING •
2

• COMMENTS •
A lightly-peated and delicately flavoured malt which makes a pleasant aperitif.

• VISITORS •
Visitors are welcome 0900–1630 Mon.–Fri., all year, and 0900–1300 Sat., May–Oct. Large parties must book in advance. Telephone 01808-511444.

At over 1000 feet above sea level, Tomatin is one of Scotland's highest distilleries. The distillery was established in 1897 and a major programme of expansion in the early 1970s made Tomatin the largest distillery in Scotland. Against a background of general decline in the industry, however, the company experienced financial difficulties in the 1980s before being bought by a Japanese consortium, thus becoming the first Scotch whisky distillery to have Japanese owners.

TOMINTOUL

**Tomintoul Distillery,
Ballindalloch, Banffshire**

• AGE •
10 years

• STRENGTH •
40%, 43%

• TASTE RATING •
2–3

• COMMENTS •
A light, delicate whisky with a fine balance of flavours in the Glenlivet style. An ideal dram for beginners, or as an aperitif.

• VISITORS •
The distillery is not open to visitors.

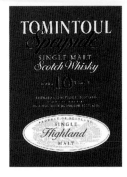

Built in 1964 near to Tomintoul, the second-highest village in Scotland and once a centre for illicit distilling, Tomintoul Distillery is also, at 1100 feet, one of the highest in the country. In spite of a scenic location, it is a modern, functional building which lacks the charm associated with the architecture of many older distilleries. Owned until 1993 by Invergordon Distillers, Tomintoul was one of the group's seven malt distilleries which passed into the hands of Whyte & Mackay that year.

SINGLE MALT

THE TORMORE

The Tormore Distillery, Advie, Grantown-on-Spey, Moray

• AGE •
10 years

• STRENGTH •
40%, 43%

• TASTE RATING •
2-3

• COMMENTS •
A medium-bodied whisky, rich and slightly nutty in flavour. An after-dinner dram.

• VISITORS •
Visitors are welcome by appointment. Telephone 01807-510244.

Built in 1959, this was Speyside's first new distillery this century. Not a traditional-looking distillery, it is an attractive complex in a pleasant Highland setting, and has the delightfully kitsch touch of a chiming clock which plays the air, *Highland Laddie*, every hour. An impressive working model of the Tormore Distillery can be seen at the Scotch Whisky Heritage Centre on Edinburgh's Royal Mile. The distillery itself is owned by Allied Distillers, with some of its produce featuring in their Long John blends.

TULLIBARDINE

**Tullibardine Distillery,
Blackford, Perthshire**

• AGE •

10 years

• STRENGTH •

40%

• TASTE RATING •

2–3

• COMMENTS •

Tullibardine is a good, all-round single malt, full-bodied and with a sweet, well-rounded flavour with a grapey note.

PRODUCT of SCOTLAND

Tullibardine

SINGLE HIGHLAND MALT
SCOTCH WHISKY

*A Single Malt Scotch Whisky of quality
and distinction distilled and bottled by*

TULLIBARDINE DISTILLERY LIMITED
BLACKFORD   PERTHSHIRE   SCOTLAND

40%vol   70cl

Tullibardine Distillery was built on the site of a medieval brewery reputed to have produced ale for the coronation of James IV in 1488. It was opened as a distillery in 1949 and is actually situated at Blackford, a few miles away from Tullibardine village. Tullibardine was one of the seven malt distilleries, previously belonging to Invergordon Distillers, which passed into the ownership of Whyte & Mackay in 1993. Since then production has been mothballed.

VAT 69

**United Distillers,
Kilmarnock, Ayrshire**

• STRENGTH •

43%

• TASTE RATING •

2-3

• COMMENTS •

A smooth, well-balanced and distinctly mature blend, light but with a pleasantly malty background.

Sandersons were Leith wine and spirit merchants who moved into whisky blending in the 1860s. William Sanderson was keen to find a notable blend to market and produced 100 different whiskies to be tested, each in numbered casks. The unanimous choice of his associates was the whisky from vat number 69, and so the name suggested itself. It was introduced onto the market in 1882. Today Sanderson and its brands are owned by United Distillers.

WALLACE

The Wallace Malt Liqueur Co.
Deanston, Perthshire

• STRENGTH •

35%

• TASTE RATING •

2

• COMMENTS •

A combination of Deanston's single malt, fruit and herbs, this rich liqueur has a delicate texture with a hint of honey

This new liqueur is named after Sir William Wallace, Guardian of Scotland, whose famous victory in 1297 over the English at the battle of Stirling Bridge took place only a few miles from Deanston Distillery, whose malt is a major component of it. Originally a cotton mill dating from 1785, Deanston was converted to a distillery in 1966 and draws it waters from the nearby River Teith. Deanston was bought by Burn Stewart of Glasgow in 1991.

WHITE HORSE

United Distillers, Glasgow

STRENGTH

43%

TASTE RATING

2-3

COMMENTS

White Horse is a smooth and distinctive whisky with peaty elements in both its aroma and flavour. It is the leading standard blend in Japan.

White Horse Distillers, known until 1924 as Mackie & Co., was established by James Logan Mackie in 1861. The company became successful under its second head, Peter Mackie, entrepreneur and the driving force who registered the name 'White Horse', called after a famous Edinburgh coaching inn, for his blend in 1890. By the time he died in 1924 his whisky was one of the foremost blends in the world. Three years later White Horse Distillers joined the Distillers Company Ltd. Today it is owned by United Distillers

WHYTE & MACKAY SPECIAL RESERVE

**Whyte & Mackay,
Glasgow**

A good quality, smooth, light-bodied whisky with a well-rounded, mellow sweetness. This is said to come from the particular blending process the company uses, vatting the component malts together in sherry butts for at least six months, and then adding the grain content before leaving the resulting blend to mature further.

James Whyte and Charles Mackay, both whisky merchants, began their partnership and blending firm in 1882. Sales and the company expanded steadily throughout the late nineteenth century and into the twentieth. The company merged with Dalmore Distillery in the 1960s, and acquired two more distilleries, Fettercairn and Tomintoul in 1972. In 1993 the Whyte & Mackay Group acquired Invergordon Distillers, adding four more malt distilleries and a grain distillery to their holdings.

BLEND

WILLIAM GRANT'S FAMILY RESERVE

Girvan Distillery, Girvan, Ayrshire

• STRENGTH •

43%

• TASTE RATING •

2

• COMMENTS •

A traditional yet individual blend of smooth character with a light, fresh taste which incorporates elements of Glenfiddich and The Balvenie.

• VISITORS •

The plant is not open to visitors.

Grants of Glenfiddich, producers of the world's biggest-selling single malt whisky, are responsible for the production of two blends: William Grant's Family Reserve and Grant's 12 Years Old, the latter being a de luxe blend. The company began as malt whisky distillers in 1887 at Glenfiddich, moving into blending and exporting in 1898. In 1962 the company built a large complex at Girvan, housing a grain distillery, a malt distillery (Ladyburn, now dismantled), and blending facilities. Blended products are bottled at a site in Paisley.

BLEND

Appendix 1: Index of malt whiskies by producing region

APPENDIX 1: MALTS BY REGION

ISLAY

LOWLANDS

Appendix 2: Miniatures

The following lists all the whiskies featured in this book and their current availability as miniatures (although not necessarily produced by the distillery). Information about miniatures can be obtained from the Mini Bottle Club (see p. 55).

A

Aberfeldy	Yes
Aberlour	Yes
An Cnoc	Yes
The Antiquary	Yes
Ardbeg	Yes
Ardmore	Yes
Auchentoshan	Yes
Aultmore	No*

B

Bailie Nicol Jarvie	Yes
Balblair	Yes
Ballentine's Finest	Yes
Balmenach	Yes
The Balvenie	Yes
Banff	Yes
Bell's Extra Special	Yes
Ben Nevis	Yes
Benriach	Yes
Benrinnes	Yes
Benromach	Yes
Big "T"	Yes

Black & White	Yes
Black Bottle	Yes
Bladnoch	Yes
Blair Athol	Yes
Bowmore	Yes
Bruichladdich	Yes
Bunnahabhain	Yes

C

Cameron Brig	No*
Caol Ila	Yes
Caperdonich	Yes
Cardhu	Yes
Chivas Regal	Yes
The Claymore	Yes
Clynelish	Yes
Coleburn	Yes
Columba Cream	Yes
Convalmore	Yes
Cragganmore	Yes
Craigellachie	Yes
Crawford's 3-Star	Yes
Cutty Sark	Yes

Cutty Sark Emerald	Yes	Glendronach	Yes
Cutty Sark Golden Jubilee	Yes	Glendullan	Yes
		Glenfarclas	Yes
		Glenfiddich	Yes

D

Dailuaine	Yes	Glen Garioch	Yes
The Dalmore	Yes	Glengoyne	Yes
Dalwhinnie	Yes	Glen Grant	Yes
Deanston	Yes	Glen Keith	Yes
Dewar's White Label	Yes	Glenkinchie	Yes
Dimple	Yes	The Glenlivet	Yes
Drambuie	Yes	Glenlochy	Yes
Dufftown	Yes	Glenlossie	Yes
Dunhill Old Master	Yes	Glen Mhor	Yes
Dunkeld Atholl Brose	Yes	Glenmorangie	Yes
		Glenmorangie PortWood	Yes

E

The Edradour	Yes	Glen Moray	Yes
		Glen Ord	Yes

F

		Glen Rosa	Yes
Fairlie's	Yes	The Glenrothes	Yes
The Famous Grouse	Yes	Glen Scotia	Yes
Fraser McDonald	Yes[†]	Glentauchers	Yes
		The Glenturret	Yes
		The Glenturret Original Malt Liq.	Yes

G

Glayva	Yes	Glenugie	Yes
Glen Albyn	Yes	Grand Macnish	Yes
Glenburgie	Yes		
Glencadam	Yes		

H

Glen Calder	Yes	Haig	Yes
Glen Deveron	Yes	Heather Cream	Yes

Highland Park	Yes

I

Immortal Memory	Yes
Imperial	Yes
Inchgower	Yes
Inchmurrin	Yes
Invergordon	Yes
Inverleven	Yes
Island Prince	Yes
Islay Mist	Yes
Isle of Jura	Yes

J

J&B Jet	Yes
J&B Rare	Yes
J&B Ultima	Yes
Johnnie Walker Black Label	Yes
Johnnie Walker Blue Label	No*
Johnnie Walker Red Label	Yes

K

Knockando	Yes

L

Lagavulin	Yes
Laphroaig	Yes
Lauder's Scotch	Yes
Ledaig	Yes
Linkwood	Yes
Littlemill	Yes
The Loch Fyne	Yes
Loch Ranza	Yes
Lochside	No
Long John	Yes
Longmorn	Yes
Longrow	Yes

M

The Macallan	Yes
Millburn	Yes
Miltonduff	Yes
Mortlach	Yes

N

North Port	Yes

O

Oban	Yes
Old Fettercairn	Yes
Old Parr	Yes
Old Pulteney	Yes
100 Hundred Pipers	Yes
The Original Mackinlay	Yes

P

Passport	Yes
Pinwinnie	Yes

Pittyvaich	Yes	Stewarts Cream of		
Port Ellen	Yes	the Barley	Yes	
Pride of Islay	Yes	Strathisla	Yes	
Pride of				
the Lowlands	Yes	**T**		
Pride of Orkney	Yes	Talisker	Yes	
Pride of Strathspey	Yes	Tamdhu	Yes	
		Tamnavulin	Yes	
R		Teacher's Highland		
Rosebank	Yes	Cream	Yes	
Royal Brackla	Yes	Teaninich	Yes	
Royal Culross	Yes	Tobermory	Yes	
Royal Lochnagar	Yes	Tomatin	Yes	
		Tomintoul	Yes	
S		The Tormore	Yes	
St Magdalene	Yes	Tullibardine	Yes	
Scapa	Yes			
Scotia Royale	Yes	**V**		
The Singleton of		VAT 69	Yes	
Auchroisk	Yes			
Speyburn	Yes	**W**		
Springbank	Yes	Wallace	Yes	
Stag's Breath		White Horse	Yes	
Liqueur	Yes	Whyte & Mackay	Yes	
Stewart Macduff	Yes	William Grant	Yes	

Notes

* These were available from the distillers as give-aways and so are not readily available to the general public.

† These are availble mainly in Italy.

COLLINS GEM

Bestselling Collins Gem titles include:

Gem English Dictionary (£3.99)

Gem Calorie Counter (£2.99)

Gem Thesaurus (£3.99)

Gem French Dictionary (£3.99)

Gem German Dictionary (£3.99)

Gem Basic Facts Mathematics (£3.50)

Gem Birds Photoguide (£3.99)

Gem Babies' Names (£3.50)

Gem Card Games (£3.50)

Gem World Atlas (£3.99)

All Collins Gems are available from your local bookseller or can be ordered directly from the publishers.

In the UK, contact Mail Order, Dept 2A, HarperCollins Publishers, Westerhill Rd, Bishopbriggs, Glasgow, G64 2QT, listing the titles required and enclosing a cheque or p.o. for the value of the books plus £1.00 for the first title and 25p for each additional title to cover p&p. Access and Visa cardholders can order on 0141-772 2281 (24 hr).

In Australia, contact Customer Services, HarperCollins Distribution, Yarrawa Rd, Moss Vale 2577 (tel. [048] 68 0300). **In New Zealand**, contact Customer Services, HarperCollins Publishers, 31 View Rd, Glenfield, Auckland 10 (tel. [09] 444 3740). **In Canada**, contact your local bookshop.

All prices quoted are correct at time of going to press.

COLLINS GEM

Other Scottish Gem titles include:

Gem Castles of Scotland

A pocket-sized guide to 100 of Scotland's most dramatic castles and strongholds **£3.99**

Gem Clans and Tartans

The histories of over 100 Scottish clans, together with colour illustrations of their tartans **£3.99**

Gem Burns Anthology

The ideal introduction to the poetry of Scotland's national bard **£3.99**

Gem Famous Scots

Illustrated biographies of over 150 famous (and infamous) Scottish men and women **£3.99**

Gem Scots Dictionary

A dictionary of the living Scots language containing over 1500 everyday words and phrases from throughout Scotland **£3.99**